THE ILLUSTRATED
LETTERS OF THE BRONTËS

THE ILLUSTRATED LETTERS OF THE BRONTËS

JULIET GARDINER

BATSFORD

FRONTISPIECE *Thomas Girtin's painting of the Yorkshire moors, Landscape with Hill and Clouds, painted in the 1790s. Compared with the paintings of Turner, Girtin's iconography of the bleak, desolate isolation of the endless expanse of the moors came not only to represent the landscape of the Brontës' lives, but its essence too, as Mrs Gaskell, Charlotte's biographer, noticed when she first met her: 'In general she sits quite alone thinking over the past ... she has the wild, strange facts of her own and her sisters' lives – and beyond and above these she has the most original and suggestive thoughts of her own: so that, like the moors, I felt on the last day as if our talk might be extended in any direction without getting to the end of any subject.'*

First published in the United Kingdom in 1992 by Collins & Brown Limited
This edition first published in the United Kingdom in 2021 by
Batsford
43 Great Ormond Street
London
WC1N 3HZ

An imprint of B. T. Batsford Holdings Limited

ISBN 978-1-84994-660-5

A CIP catalogue record for this book is available from the British Library.

10 9 8 7 6 5 4 3 2

Reproduction by Rival Colour, UK
Printed and bound by Toppan Printing International Ltd, China

This book can be ordered direct from the publisher at www.batsfordbooks.com

CONTENTS

INTRODUCTION

'WHEN MY CHILDREN WERE VERY YOUNG,' recalled the Reverend Patrick Brontë, '… as far as I can remember, the oldest was about ten years of age, and the youngest about four, thinking that they knew more than I had discerned, in order to make them speak with less timidity, I deemed that if they were put under a sort of cover I might gain my end; and happening to have a mask in the house, I told them to stand and speak boldly from under the cover of the mask.'

The poetry and novels of Charlotte, Emily and Anne Brontë have often been portrayed as the masks through which these daughters of the Parsonage spoke with 'less timidity', and revealed that they knew – and gave voice to – a great deal that others had not discovered about them, nor could imagine how they had discovered for themselves, given the narrow confines of their restricted lives.

In recounting the lives of the Brontës – 'such a life as I never heard of before', according to Charlotte's biographer, Mrs Gaskell – it is rewarding to listen to the many voices in which they wrote. For the solitary lives which the three sisters and their brother, Branwell, lived with their austere clergyman father and reticent aunt, in the isolated, moor-lapped grey stone Parsonage at Haworth in Yorkshire, threw them for lengthy periods of time almost entirely into each other's company, voracious reading and protean writing.

The primary direct source for the Brontës' lives is Charlotte's correspondence. Apart from the sisters' tragic first schooldays at Cowan Bridge, it was Charlotte who ventured first and most frequently into the 'world without'. From Roe Head, where she went as a pupil in January 1831, Charlotte wrote only two known letters, one to her brother Branwell – 'as usual I address my weekly letter to you, because to you I find the most to say' – but it was at Roe Head that she made two friends who were to become her lifelong correspondents: Ellen Nussey and Mary Taylor. They were entirely different in background and outlook and

The Brontë sisters in a group portrait painted by Branwell, c.1834, known as the 'pillar portrait'. The space between Anne and Emily (far left and left) and Charlotte (right) was originally occupied by Branwell. At some point the artist painted himself out of his own portrait. The reason is not known. Perhaps Branwell was dissatisfied with his representation of his own face; perhaps he no longer felt the equal of his grave-faced sisters or part of their world. The oil painting was further damaged when it was cut from its frame by Charlotte's husband, the Reverend Arthur Bell Nicholls, and taken back to Ireland with him after Patrick Brontë's death, where it lay folded in a drawer for many years.

Charlotte's relationship with each of them was different. To Mary, who was of the radical political persuasion of her family, independent, intelligent and outspoken, appealing to the rebellious side of Charlotte's complex nature, only one letter survives, a long epistle Charlotte wrote after her friend had emigrated to New Zealand in 1845, about the first visit she and Anne had paid to her publishers in London. But something of the tenor of the correspondence can be gained from Mary's response to the receipt of a copy of *Jane Eyre* in 1848:

> IT SEEMED TO ME INCREDIBLE that you had actually written a book. Such events did not happen when I was in England. I begin to believe in your existence much as I do in Mr Rochester's. In a believing mood I don't doubt either of them … You are very different from me in having no doctrine to preach. It is impossible to squeeze a moral out of your production. Has the world gone so well with you that you have no protest to make against its absurdities? Did you never sneer or declaim in your first sketches? I will scold you well when I see you.

But Mary Taylor never had that opportunity; Charlotte died five years before she returned to England.

Charlotte first wrote to Ellen Nussey from Haworth during her first school holidays from Roe Head; her last letter was a scribbled pencil note from her deathbed. In the years between, hundreds of letters passed between the friends, and it is these which remain the chief source for the life of the Brontës. Charlotte wrote to Ellen of the small details of her daily life and that of her family; she wrote of her resentments at having to seek her living as a governess, all the privations that that entailed, and her envy of Ellen's independence, her thoughts on the position of women, her feelings towards her sisters, her paralyzing grief at their deaths, her disappointment with her brother Branwell, who had 'set off to seek his fortune in the wild, wandering, adventurous, romantic, knight-errant-like capacity of clerk on the Leeds and Manchester Railroad', which soon turned to

OPPOSITE *An 1822 map of the West Riding of Yorkshire – the world of the Brontës. It shows Keighley, the nearest town, some four miles from Haworth, where the villagers had to go to seek 'medical advice, for stationery, books, law, dress or dainties', and where the Brontës walked to borrow books from the Mechanics' Institute library; Bradford, the nearest city, where Branwell tried to make his living as a portrait painter; Guiseley, where Patrick and Maria Brontë were married; Mirfield, where Charlotte went to school at Roe Head; Birstall, where Ellen Nussey, the friend she met at Roe Head lived; Thornton, where Patrick Brontë was curate from 1815 to 1820 and where Charlotte, Emily, Branwell and Anne were born; and Haworth itself, where 'there were shopkeepers for the humbler and everyday wants', and where Charlotte, Branwell, Emily and Anne Brontë spent nearly their entire lives.*

despair. She described her depressions, her feelings of worthlessness and her religious crises, her loneliness, her sense of duty towards God and towards her father, and her feelings about love and about marriage, including her eventual marriage to the Reverend Arthur Bell Nicholls. She did not write to Ellen, who she recognized was 'no more than a conscientious, observant, calm, well-bred Yorkshire girl', of her inner life, the imagination that informed her writing, for she knew that:

> I AM NOT LIKE YOU. If you knew my thoughts; the dreams that absorb me; and the fiery imagination that at times eats me up and makes me feel Society as it is, wretchedly insipid, you would pity and I dare say despise me.

A few months after her marriage in 1854, Charlotte wrote to Ellen:

> ARTHUR [BELL NICHOLLS] has been glancing over this note. He thinks I have written too freely … Men don't seem to understand making letters a vehicle of communication,

they always seem to think us incautious. I'm sure I don't think I have said anything rash; however you must BURN it when read. Arthur says such letters as mine never ought to be kept, they are as dangerous as lucifer matches, so be sure to follow a recommendation he has just given, 'fire them' or 'there will be no more', such is his resolve … give him a plain pledge to that effect, or he will read every line I write and elect himself censor of our correspondence …

Ellen gave him her pledge, but she did not destroy the letters.

As well as her letters to Ellen, Charlotte wrote home to Emily during her year in Brussels expressing her unhappiness, but not the real reasons for that unhappiness; she wrote to her family from her various posts as a governess; she corresponded with friends she had made in Brussels and with her old headmistress from Roe Head, Miss Wooler. After the publication of *Jane Eyre* she replied to letters and reviews from the famous: G. H. Lewes, William Makepeace Thackeray, Harriet Martineau, Mrs Gaskell; and whenever she undertook a trip to London, or a visit to her new-found literary friends, she wrote to her father about it. But in her later years, the person with whom Charlotte struck up a correspondence, equal in some ways in intimacy, but more concerned with writerly things, to that which she had with Ellen Nussey, was the reader at her publisher at Smith, Elder & Co., William Smith Williams, and to a considerable extent also with the head of the firm, George Smith. Although she always addressed her letters to both 'My Dear Sir', and signed them 'respectfully' or 'sincerely', perhaps it was to her publishers that a self-observation Charlotte had made many years earlier best applied: 'I cannot be formal in a letter. If I write at all I must write as I think.'

On 16 April 1855, Charlotte's friend of her brief years of fame, the novelist Mrs Gaskell, received an entirely unexpected letter from Patrick Brontë:

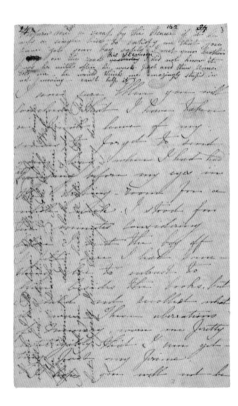

OPPOSITE *Charlotte Brontë, painted sometime after 1840 by J. H. Thompson, a Bradford artist and friend of her brother, Branwell, from whom he seems to have borrowed money and run up considerable debts 'of which my father and Aunt had no knowledge'.*

OPPOSITE *A letter Charlotte wrote in her characteristic slanting hand to her friend Ellen Nussey on 6 December 1836, on returning to teach at Miss Wooler's school at Roe Head where she and Ellen had met as pupils in 1831. Charlotte has crosshatched the page with two sets of lines, possibly to save paper, but perhaps more probably out of consideration to Ellen since, prior to Rowland Hill's Penny Post of 1840 which introduced a uniform postal rate paid in advance, letter were charged by the page to the recipient rather than the sender.*

FINDING A GREAT MANY SCRIBBLERS ... have published articles in newspapers and tracts – respecting my dear daughter Charlotte ... and seeing that many things that have been stated are true, but more false ... I can see no better plan under the circumstances than to apply to some established Author to write a brief account of her life – and to make some remarks on her works. You seem to me to be best qualified for doing what I wish should be done.

Mrs Gaskell had already been thinking of doing exactly that and so she immediately acquiesced in the Reverend Brontë's 'impetuous wish' to make his daughter's life known. Apart from the help from the Parsonage, Ellen Nussey contributed her memories of Charlotte, and lent Mrs Gaskell the 350 letters she had failed to destroy; Mary Taylor sent a long reminiscence from New Zealand; and other friends and acquaintances of Charlotte, servants of the family and the Haworth stationer, John Greenwood, shared their recollections and opinions. Mrs Gaskell ventured to Brussels where Mme Heger refused to see her, but M. Heger politely sketched his recollections of his two difficult English pupils, Emily and Charlotte. (He also showed Mrs Gaskell Charlotte's letters to him, but, aware of the pain this could cause, she did not allude to them in her *Life*.) All these, added to the conversations she had had with Charlotte herself, and her letters, are the substance of Mrs Gaskell's *Life of Charlotte Brontë*, which was published in March 1857 to a chorus of praise, with the *Athenaeum* declaring: 'As a work of Art, we do not recollect the life of a woman by a woman so well executed.' Published, as it was, so soon after Charlotte's death, it is properly part of the Brontë story.

Writing to her publisher after Emily's death, Charlotte recounted how her sister declined to go out, saying 'What is the use? Charlotte will bring it home to me.' And as Charlotte in many ways reported the world to her sisters, so she interpreted her sisters to the world. She was the first artificer of the Brontë legend, interposing herself between the memory of her family and their critics. There are only a scattering of short letters from Emily and Anne, mostly notes to Charlotte's friend Ellen Nussey, and a collection of often rambling, frequently raw and urgent, and sometimes lachrymose epistles from Branwell. We read of Emily, Anne and Branwell in the margins of Charlotte's much better-documented life. But it is also possible to reclaim Emily and Anne from sources other than those refracted through the lens of Charlotte's letters and commentaries, valuable though these are.

Emily and Anne wrote joint diary papers every four years of their adult lives. These moving documents, found after the sisters' deaths, folded into a tiny black box, two or three inches long, used for pins, perhaps, or snuff, take a sounding of their lives on Emily's birthday and intermingle a jumble of recent family events and that day's happenings with projections and questions about the coming years in the lives both of the Brontë family and of the inhabitants of the imaginary lands of Gondal and Gaaldine which they created. These were the territories which Emily and Anne mapped from a potent mixture of facts and images garnered from paintings, books, newspapers and periodicals, just as Charlotte and Branwell created Angria from the same material. The poems, plays, stories and miniature magazines, which they wrote for and about their countries of the mind, have familiar landmarks: the Niger Delta, the Duke of Wellington, Byron, Queen Victoria herself; but these were colonized, transformed and vivified by the children's imagination and present an alternative narrative of their childhood, the 'web of sunny air' they spun out of their quiet, restricted lives, as Charlotte showed in bidding farewell to Angria and her favourite character, Zamorna:

I OWE HIM SOMETHING, *he has held*
A lofty, burning lamp to me
Whose rays surrounding darkness quelled
And showed me wonders shadow free.

The 'gun group' portrait, an oil painting of the Brontë children by Branwell, c.1833. A photograph of the original of this painting has been discovered showing the picture in a poor condition; previously only a fragment of Emily in profile believed to be from this portrait was known (see page 71). It is conjectured that Arthur Nicholls found the painting a poor likeness of his wife Charlotte, Anne and Branwell, and destroyed the picture, saving only the portrait of Emily. This engraving is from a copy published in J. Horsfall Turner's Haworth Past and Present *(1879).*

The books and poems that Charlotte, Emily and Anne wrote when they grew up were likewise based on familiar landmarks and experiences, and whilst not being narrowly autobiographical – 'You are not to suppose any of the characters in *Shirley* intended as literal portraits,' Charlotte wrote to Ellen Nussey. 'It would not suit the rules of art, nor my own feelings to write in that style. We only suffer reality to suggest, never to dictate' – the three sisters wove those experiences into works which addressed the central concerns of their lives as women. Charlotte drew an implicit contrast between her writing and that of Jane Austen on reading *Emma* in 1850:

> HER BUSINESS IS not half so much with the human heart as with the human eyes, mouth, hands and feet; what sees keenly, speaks aptly, moves flexibly, it suits her to study, but what throbs fast and fully, though hidden, what blood rushes through, what is the unseen seat of Life and the sentient target of death – this Miss Austen ignores …

That was not the Brontë way. Emily wrote:

> NO COWARD SOUL *is mine*
> *No trembler in the world's storm-troubled sphere*

And Charlotte wrote in *Jane Eyre*:

> WOMEN ARE SUPPOSED to be very calm generally, but women feel just as men feel … they suffer from too rigid a restraint, too absolute a stagnation, precisely as men would suffer; and it is narrow-minded in their more privileged fellow creatures to say that they ought to confine themselves to making puddings and knitting stockings, to playing the piano and embroidering bags. It is thoughtless to condemn them, or laugh at them, if they seek to do more or learn more than custom had pronounced necessary for their sex.

And throughout their lives Charlotte, Emily and Anne Brontë did 'do more', in their writings: their letters, their juvenilia, their diaries and private papers, their poems and their seven published novels.

CHAPTER 1
THE ROAD TO HAWORTH

'I DO NOT DENY', wrote the Reverend Patrick Brontë to Mrs Gaskell on the publication of her *Life* of his daughter Charlotte in 1857, in which she had painted a less than flattering portrait of him, 'that I am somewhat eccentrick [sic]. Had I been numbered amongst the calm, sedate, concentric men of the world, I should not have been as I am now, and I should, in all probability, never have had such children as mine have been.'

The man who was to father three daughters of genius was born on the day of the saint after whom he was named, 17 March 1777, the oldest of the ten children of Eleanor (or Alice, as she was often called) and Hugh Brunty, a farmhand of Drumballyroney, in County Down, Ireland.

He sketched his life for Mrs Gaskell:

> SINCE, AT MR NICHOLLS' REQUEST and mine, you have kindly consented to give a brief account of my daughter Charlotte's life, I will state a few facts which, as her biographer, you might wish to know. For the gratification of those who might be desirous of knowing anything of me, I will in as few words as I can gratify their curiosity. My father's name was Hugh Brontë. He was a native of the south of Ireland, and was left an orphan at an early age. It was said that he was of ancient family. Whether this was or was not so I never gave myself the trouble to inquire, since his lot in life as well as mine depended, under providence, not on family descent but our own exertions. He came to the north of Ireland, and made an early but suitable marriage. His pecuniary means were small – but, renting a few acres of land, he and my mother by dint of application and industry managed to bring up a family of ten children in a respectable manner.

Mrs Gaskell added her own observations to these bare facts, noting how 'early [Patrick] gave tokens of extraordinary quickness and intelligence. He had also his

OPPOSITE *The Mountains of Mourne, which were visible from the window of the earth-floored, whitewashed, two-roomed cottage in Drumballyroney, County Down, where Patrick Brontë (then Brunty) was born on St Patrick's Day, 17 March 1777. The wild beauty of the mountains, slate blue in the distance, was a great attraction to Patrick who walked in the foothills and was pleased to find an echoing wildness in the Yorkshire moors when he came as a curate to Haworth.*

ABOVE *An illustration from John Bunyan's* The Pilgrim's Progress *(1678–1684), one of the three books to be found in Patrick Brontë's childhood home. Charlotte took the allegory of the pilgrim's struggle as a text for Jane Eyre's spiritual and moral 'journey' towards an earthly paradise in Mr Rochester's house.*

LEFT *Patrick's love of God found expression in the magnificent landscape of his native land, but once in England studying for the ministry, he knew he would never live there again – he only paid one brief visit to his Celtic homeland in 1806 after his ordination.*

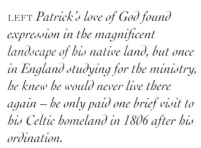

full share of ambition.' It was an ambition which had taken root in the cottage, with a corn kiln in the back room which Hugh Brunty used to supplement his meagre income. The family had moved there from the mud-floored hovel where Patrick had been born. Of necessity, they led a simple life, with plain fare of buttermilk and bread made from a mixture of Fadge potatoes and oatmeal; this induced heartburn in the young Patrick and, he thought, caused the dyspepsia that dogged his adult life.

The Bruntys wore only woollen clothes made from wool spun, dyed and carded by Eleanor. Hugh had a fear of fire and forbade the wearing of linen or cotton, a fear which was never to leave his son Patrick, who was to insist on buckets of water on the landing in his own family's home. It was not until Charlotte was a married woman that Patrick's prejudices were disregarded and curtains were hung at the Parsonage windows at Haworth.

But although Hugh and Eleanor Brunty were virtually illiterate and gained what little knowledge they had of literature from the telling of Irish folk tales and hearing passages read aloud from books – perhaps by a visiting preacher or local schoolmaster – there were books on the cottage shelf: four. Patrick's mother had her own small copy of the New Testament, whilst his father's library consisted of the Bible, the poems of Robert Burns and John Bunyan's *The Pilgrim's Progress*, a work Patrick soon knew almost by heart.

A book was always in his hands as he trudged to his work as a linen weaver, and soon it was to be a volume that he had bought for himself with some hard-earned savings on the day that he was sent on an errand for his employer to Belfast: Milton's *Paradise Lost*. Indeed it was the boy's devotion to reading, and his tendency to declaim passages aloud as he walked along, that caught the attention of the man who was to become his first mentor, Andrew Harshaw, a Presbyterian minister and teacher, who gave Patrick the run of his library. Soon, Patrick was denying himself sleep and devouring the works of Ovid, Virgil, Homer and Herodotus, ruining his eyes for life with the poor light afforded him by a flickering rush. In 1793, Harshaw recommended his young protégé for a position at Glascar Hill Presbyterian School, where Patrick taught for five years, introducing the children of local rural families to a study of literature, history and the classics and sharing with them his passion for nature on long rambles in the nearby Mountains of Mourne.

In the autumn of 1798, the Reverend Thomas Tighe, a notable Methodist minister and friend of John Wesley, offered Patrick – now twenty-one and grown tall and angular, with auburn hair and intense, pale blue eyes – promotion. He was to teach at the much larger school at Drumballyroney, and tutor Tighe's own children as well. It was whilst in this household that the young Brontë made a momentous decision; his ability as a teacher, his sense of awe at the natural world (a wonder which he was to instil in his daughter Emily) and his growing interest in and knowledge of theology, led in one direction: the pulpit.

In September 1802, with the £25 he had managed to save, Patrick Brontë set sail for England and Tighe's old college, St John's, Cambridge. After he left Ireland to serve God in England, Patrick returned home only once, though he sent his mother money scrimped from his earnings all her life; and he never brought his children to see their father's homeland. It was not until Charlotte married another Irish clergyman, the Reverend Arthur Bell Nicholls, that she was to pay a visit to Ireland, only months before she died. But the legacy of Ireland was deep within Patrick: the wild beauty of the Mountains of Mourne which drew him

OPPOSITE *The library at St John's College, Cambridge. Patrick Brontë entered St John's – Wordsworth and Coleridge's alma mater – on 1 October 1802. The college was also where his mentor, the Reverend Thomas Tighe, had been an undergraduate and it had a reputation for its strong representation in the divinity faculty. It was also 'noted for its preponderance of Yorkshiremen'. Whilst at St John's Patrick enlisted as a volunteer in the civilian corps, training with weapons to resist a possible Napoleonic invasion from across the Channel. One of his fellows-in-arms was the youthful Lord Palmerston, later to become prime minister.*

to find their counterpart in the Yorkshire moors; the language and romance of Ireland, which he wove into his own poetry and into the Celtic myths and stories which he would recount to his children and which had such an effect on them all, Emily in particular; and the sense of apartness which was the topography of the young Brontës' world. Although when Mrs Gaskell first met Patrick in the 1850s 'he spoke with no trace of an Irish accent', there were those Yorkshiremen who remembered that when he took his curacy at Dewsbury some forty years earlier, Patrick strode the parish in an Ulsterman's blue linen frock coat, a shillelagh (or staff) in his hand, and spoke with a strong Irish accent. His mother had been a Roman Catholic who had converted to Protestantism on marriage. Patrick was to become a member of the evangelical wing of the Anglican Church, whose clergy were strongly influenced by Methodism but dedicated to keeping their fire within the established Church as an antidote to popish ways. Among the young blades of Cambridge, Patrick rarely referred to his peasant background and he had to eke out his savings by working as a sizar, 'fagging' for the wealthier students, until, thankfully, through the good agencies of the reformer William Wilberforce, he secured an annuity of £10.

It was while he was studying theology and classics at Cambridge that Patrick changed his name, first to Branty, then to Bronté, finally settling on Brontë, possibly following the example of one of his heroes, Lord Nelson, who had had that name bestowed upon him by the King of Naples.

In 1806 Patrick took Holy Orders in the Anglican Church and embarked on a series of curacies, taking up duties at Weathersfield in Essex, then Shrewsbury in Shropshire, before going to Yorkshire in 1809, first to Dewsbury, to serve as curate to the Reverend Buckworth, a hymn-writer of some acclaim ('Great God and wilt thou condescend/To be my Father and my Friend?'), and then, in 1811, moving to Hartshead, a few miles away. It was here that the thirty-five-year-old curate met his future wife, Maria Branwell, a Cornishwoman from Penzance,

ABOVE *Patrick was admitted to St John's as a sizar, or servitor, to his more affluent fellow students, which reduced his fees both to the college and to the University of Cambridge. In addition, Patrick became an exhibitioner, the recipient of a fund established 'for thirty of the poorest and best disposed scholars', and received help from the Church Missionary Society Fund, an organization directed towards promoting promising recruits to the Church.*

BELOW *Woodhouse Grove, at Apperley Bridge, near Bradford, housed a school for the education of the sons of Wesleyan ministers. Its first headmaster, John Fennell, appointed Patrick Brontë, then a curate at Hartshead, some ten miles away, as an inspector to examine the pupils in Latin and the scriptures. Invited to dine with his employer, Patrick met Fennell's niece, Maria Branwell, who had just arrived at the school to help out with the school's sewing and mending, and to act as a companion to her cousin Jane.*

who was on a visit to her uncle, John Fennell, a Yorkshire Methodist lay preacher and headmaster. She was, according to Mrs Gaskell:

EXTREMELY SMALL IN PERSON, not pretty but very elegant and always dressed with a great simplicity of taste, which accorded well with her general character, and of which some of her details call to mind the style of dress preferred by her daughter for her favourite heroines. Mr Brontë was soon captivated by this little, gentle creature, and this time declared it was for life.

Nearly thirty years later, Maria's daughter, Charlotte, had the opportunity to evoke this 'little, gentle creature', as she recalled in a letter she wrote to a friend on 16 February 1850:

A FEW DAYS SINCE, a little incident occurred which curiously touched me. Papa put into my hands a little packet of letters and papers telling me that they were mamma's, and that I might read them. I did read them, in a frame of mind I cannot describe. The papers were yellow with time, all having been written before I was born. It was strange now to peruse for the first time, the records of a mind whence my own sprang: and most strange, and at once sad and sweet, to find that a mind of a truly fine, pure and elevated order. They were written to Papa before they were married. There is a rectitude, a refinement, a constancy, a modesty, a sense of gentleness about them that is indescribable. I wish she had lived and that I had known her.

The letters of Maria to Patrick – none of his to her remain – show a sensible young woman (Maria was twenty-nine when she met her future husband) with a strong sense of religious duty and piety – indeed Maria's own writing was confined to an unpublished tract, *The Advantages of Poverty in Religious Concerns*, which Patrick endorsed after her death: 'The above was written by my dear wife, and is for insertion in one of the

LEFT *Penzance, Cornwall, home of Maria Branwell. Though 'sufficiently well descended' to mix in good society, she jumped at her aunt's invitation to Yorkshire.*

OPPOSITE, TOP *Maria Branwell as a young woman, an unattributed portrait. Maria was twenty-nine, a gentle, religious woman, recently orphaned and with an annuity of £50, when she met Patrick. He was soon 'captivated by this little, gentle creature, and this time declared that it was for life'.*

OPPOSITE, BOTTOM *Patrick Brontë as a young man. When Maria met him he 'had the reputation in the neighbourhood of being a very handsome fellow, full of Irish enthusiasm, and with something of an Irishman's capability of falling easily in love.'*

periodical publications. Keep it as a memorial of her.' They also show someone of an ardent, loving – and sometimes teasing – spirit, and afford us a glimpse of the possibilities of happiness for 'My dear saucy Pat', as Maria once addressed her betrothed, which the subsequent years of suffering were to cloud:

> NOW DON'T YOU THINK that you deserve this epithet, far more, than I do that which you have given me? [It is believed that Patrick had sneaked a kiss from Maria] I really know not what to make of your last; the winds, waves, and rocks almost stunned me. I thought you were giving me the account of some terrible dream, or that you had the presentiment of the fate of my poor box [the boat carrying a trunk of Maria's possessions from Cornwall to Yorkshire had been smashed on to rocks in a storm at sea, and all her books, clothes and trinkets had been lost], having no idea that your lively imagination could make so much of the slight reproof conveyed in my last. What will you say when you get a *real, downright scolding*?

But even though he left no love letters. we know that Patrick was a wordsmith too, as his poem 'Lines, addressed to a Lady, on her Birth-Day', written for Maria at thirty, proves:

> *SWEET IS THE APRIL MORN …*
> *Maria let us walk, and breathe, the morning air,*
> *And hear the cuckoo sing …*
> *The modest daisy and the violet blue,*
> *Inviting, spread their charms for you.*
> *How much enhanced is all this bliss to me,*
> *Since it is shared, in mutual joy with thee! …*

He was also adept at recounting tales of Ireland and of his moral beliefs in works like *The Rural Minstrel, The Cottage in the Woods: or The Art of Becoming Rich and Happy* – a sort of spiritual answer to Richardson's worldly novel, *Pamela* – and *The*

Maid of Killarney: or Albion and Flora: a modern tale; in which are interwoven some cursory remarks on Religion and Politics – his best work, which gives an insight into some of the family's later behaviour: why the Brontë children were so reluctant to eat meat; why Charlotte never learned to dance until she went to Brussels; and why Branwell's imbroglios with the low life of Yorkshire caused such consternation at the Parsonage.

Maria and Patrick were married on 29 December 1812, at Guiseley, in a double ceremony with Jane Fennell, Maria's cousin, and William Morgan, Patrick's friend, on the same day that Maria's sister, Charlotte, was married in Penzance. Maria's niece, another Charlotte, gave an account of her aunt's wedding:

> JANE FENNELL was previously engaged to the Rev. William Morgan. And when the time arrived for their marriage, Mr Fennell said he should not have to give his daughter and niece away, and if so, he could not marry them; so it was arranged that Mr Morgan should marry Mr Brontë and Maria Branwell, and afterwards Mr Brontë should provide the same kindly office towards Mr Morgan and Jane Fennell. So the bridegrooms married each other and the brides acted as bridesmaids to each other. My father and mother, Joseph and Charlotte Branwell, were married at Madron, and that was then the parish church of Penzance, on the same day and hour. Perhaps a similar case never happened before or since: two sisters and four first cousins being united in holy matrimony at one and the same time. And they were all happy marriages. Mr Brontë was perhaps peculiar, but I have always heard my own dear mother say that he was devotedly fond of his wife, and she of him.

The newly-weds made their first home at Clough Lane, Hightown, and it was here that the Brontës' first two children were born: Maria, named for her mother, in 1814; and Elizabeth, called after her mother's sister, on 8 February 1815. In the same year, Patrick was appointed to a living at Thornton, near Bradford, where Charlotte, also named after a sister of Maria's, was born on 21 April 1816. An only son, Patrick Branwell, incorporating the names of both parents, followed on

OPPOSITE *The Welsh clergyman William Morgan, whom Patrick Brontë met in 1809 when they were both curates in Shropshire. Morgan married Patrick and Maria, christened four of their children, and officiated at the funeral of Maria and three of the Brontë children. He married Maria's cousin Jane Fennell.*

RIGHT *The Yorkshire Moors. Mrs Gaskell described how 'all round the horizon there is the same line of sinuous wave-like hills; the scoops into which they fall only revealing other hills beyond, of similar colour and shape, crowned with wild, bleak moors – grand from ideas of solitude and loneliness which they suggest, or oppressive from the feeling which they give of being pent-up by some monotonous and illimitable barrier according to the mood of mind in which the spectator may be.' During the Brontës' lifetime, the Yorkshire moors, unlike the Lake District, were not considered to be romantic: it is partly the prose of* Wuthering Heights *that has infused the bleak wastes with the dramatic appeal they have today.*

26 June 1817; Emily Jane (Jane after her godmother, Jane Fennell, and Emily for herself alone) on 30 July 1818; and the last child, Anne, named for her maternal grandmother and her father's sister, was born on 17 January 1820.

A few months later, seven heavily laden carts lumbered slowly up the cobbled streets of Haworth six miles away, 'bearing the new parson's household goods for his new abode'. The Reverend Brontë was removing his wife and six small children to a new parish. It was a tribute to Patrick's ministry that he had been offered the living at Haworth, for a previous incumbent, the great eighteenth-century preacher William Grimshaw, had made this windswept Pennine parish the stronghold of the powerful Evangelical religious revival centred on Yorkshire.

It was, Mrs Gaskell tells us, a fairly prosperous town:

THE PEOPLE OF HAWORTH were none of them very poor. Many of them were employed in the neighbouring worsted mills; a few were mill-owners and manufacturers in a small way; there were also some shop-keepers for the humbler and everyday wants; but for medical advice, for stationery, books, law, dress, or dainties, the inhabitants had to go to Keighley …

[It] is a long, straggling village: one steep narrow street – so steep that the flagstones with which it is paved are placed endways, that the horses' feet may have something to cling to, and not slip down backwards, which if they did they would soon reach Keighley.

But it was not a healthy place, despite its elevated position 800 feet up in the Pennines. There were no sewers and the water was polluted, contributing to a high mortality rate: the average age of death in Haworth was twenty-five; 41 per cent of babies died before reaching their first birthday.

At the apex of the village, on the very edge of the moors, stood the Parsonage, which was to be home for the Brontës for the rest of all their lives. It was a rectangular house, of typical Georgian design with a pedimented portico, built in 1779 of limestone grit, as were most of the other dwellings in Haworth, a stone that soon weathers to a sombre shade of grey. 'One wonders', reflected Mrs Gaskell, 'how the bleak aspect of her new home – the low, oblong stone parsonage, high up, yet with a still higher backdrop of sweeping moors – struck on the gentle, delicate wife [Maria] whose health was even then failing.'

Ellen Nussey, Charlotte's schoolfriend and lifelong correspondent and confidante, recalls a visit she made to the Parsonage in 1833 during the school holidays:

THERE WAS NOT MUCH CARPET ANYWHERE except in the sitting-room [which Charlotte herself always referred to as 'the dining room'], and on the study floor [designated by the Brontës as 'the parlour']. The hall floor and stairs were done with

RIGHT *Haworth in the West Riding of Yorkshire was at the centre of a wool-producing area, with sheep grazing the moors. Young children worked in the wool trade in cottage industries and factories, and it was not until the 1833 Factory Act – nineteen years after this picture of factory children was published – that the hours of children between nine and thirteen were limited to forty-eight a week, children under nine were banned from most mills and part-time education for factory children was required.*

OPPOSITE *Emily Jane Brontë's christening mug. Emily was christened by the Reverend William Morgan at St James's Church, Thornton, on 20 August 1818. Her godparents included John and Jane Fennell (Jane was Maria Brontë's cousin). A china beaker like this was a traditional nineteenth-century christening gift.*

sand-stone, always beautifully clean, as everything was about the house; the walls were not papered, but stained in a pretty dove-coloured tint; hair-seated chairs and mahogany tables, book-shelves in the study, but not many of these elsewhere. Scant and bare indeed, many will say, yet it was not a scantness that made itself felt. Mind and thought, I had almost said elegance, but certainly refinement, diffused themselves over all and made nothing really wanting.

At the bottom of the treeless garden lay the Church of St Michael and All Angels with its three-tiered pulpit. It was from here that the Reverend Grimshaw had preached his rousing sermons the century before, and from here that the Reverend Brontë would, each Sunday, address his congregation, who, recalls Ellen Nussey:

ASSEMBLED, APPARENTLY TO LISTEN. They sat in, or leaned, in their pews; some few, perhaps, were resting, after a long walk over the moors. The children, many of them in clogs (or sabots), pattered in from school after service had commenced, and pattered out again before the sermon. The sexton, with a long staff, continually walked around in the aisles, 'knobbing' sleepers when he dare, shaking his head at and threatening unruly children; but when the sermon began, there was a change. Attitudes took the listening forms, eyes were turned on the preacher. It was curious, now, to note the expression. A rustic, untaught intelligence gleamed in their faces; in some, a daring, doubting, questioning look, as if they would like to offer some defiant objection. Mr Brontë always addressed his hearers in extempore style. Very often he selected a parable from one of the Gospels, which he explained in the simplest manner – sometimes going over his own words and explaining them also, so as to be perfectly intelligible to the lowest comprehension … The parishioners respected Mr Brontë because, as one of them said, 'he's a grand man; he lets other folks' business alone'. No doubt Mr Brontë's knowledge of human nature made him aware that this was the best course to pursue, till their independence had acquired a more civilized standard.

To the side of the house, through a small gate in the wall, was the graveyard, where some 40,000 lay buried under a jumble of slab tombs, 'a dreary, dreary, place,' described a friend of Mrs Gaskell, 'literally *paved* with rain-blackened tomb-stones'. The moors bore down behind the house, an endless expanse of heather, bracken, ling, bilberry, moss and grass stretching as far as the eye could see, changing colour with the seasons. It was broken near the house by series of irregular dry-stone walls, inadequate breakers when 'on autumnal or winter nights, the four winds of heaven seemed to meet and rage together, tearing round the house as if they were wild beasts trying to find an entrance.'

Haworth Parsonage. An illustration from Mrs Gaskell's The Life of Charlotte Brontë *in which she describes the Brontës' home: 'The parsonage stands at right angles to the road; so that, in fact, parsonage, church and belfried school-house form three sides of an irregular oblong of which the fourth is open to the fields and moors that lie beyond … The house is of grey stone, two storeys high, heavily roofed with flags, in order to resist the winds that might strip off a lighter covering … Everything about the place tells of a most dainty order, the most exquisite cleanliness. The door-steps are spotless; the small old-fashioned window panes glitter like looking-glass. Inside and outside of that house cleanliness goes up into its essence, purity.'*

But the family were not to be together in their new home for long.
On 27 November 1821, Patrick Brontë wrote to his good friend and former
colleague, the Reverend John Buckworth:

MY DEAR WIFE was taken dangerously ill on 29 January last: and a little more than
seven months afterwards, she died. During every week and almost every day of this
long tedious interval I expected her final removal. For the first three months
I was left nearly quite alone, unless you can suppose my six little children and
nurse and servants to have been company. Had I been at D[ewsbury]
I should not have wanted kind friends; had I been at H[artshead] I should
have seen others occasionally; or had I been at T[hornton] a family who
were ever truly kind would have soothed my sorrows; but I was at
H[aworth], a stranger in a strange land …

Some years later, a servant told Mrs Gaskell that from the
moment Mrs Brontë had been

CONFINED TO THE BEDROOM from which she would never come
forth alive … you would not have known there was a child in the
house, they were such still, noiseless, good little creatures. Maria
would shut herself up (Maria but seven!) in the children's study with
a newspaper, and be able to tell one everything when she came out;
debates in parliament and I don't know what all. She was as good as
a mother to her sisters and brother. But there never were such good
children. I used to think them spiritless, they were so different to any
children I had ever seen.

Mrs Gaskell then recounted:

> THE MOTHER WAS NOT very anxious to see much of her children,
> probably because the sight of them, knowing they were soon to be motherless,
> would have agitated her too much.

As she died in her upstairs room, Maria Brontë's despairing last words, 'Oh God my poor children, oh God my poor children', had echoed through the quiet house in September 1821, less than eighteen months after moving to Haworth. As Mrs Gaskell sympathized:

> THE LIVES OF THOSE QUIET CHILDREN must have become quieter and lonelier
> still. Charlotte tried hard, in after years, to recall the remembrance of her mother
> and could bring back two or three pictures of her. One was when, sometime in the
> evening light, she had been playing with her little boy, Patrick Branwell, in the
> parlour of Haworth parsonage. But the recollections of four and five years old
> are of a very fragmentary character.

Two months later, seeking a mother for his 'innocent prattling children', Patrick Brontë proposed marriage to a family friend, Elizabeth Firth. Politely, but firmly, she declined.

The next spring, the widower wrote to the mother of a woman he had courted, but been discouraged by her family from marrying, when he was the curate of Weathersfield in Essex. Receiving no satisfactory reply, he addressed his suit to the daughter:

> I EXPERIENCED A VERY AGREEABLE SENSATION in my heart, at this moment, on
> reflecting that you are *still* single, and am so selfish as to wish you to remain so, even if
> you would never allow me to see you. *You* were the *first* whose hand I solicited, and no
> doubt I was the *first* to whom *you promised to give that hand*.

OPPOSITE *Charlotte's reworking of the portrait of her mother. She had 'tried hard, in after years, to recall … her mother and could bring back two or three pictures of her', and in this idealized portrait of Maria, who was 'not pretty; but very elegant and always dressed with a quiet simplicity of taste which accorded well with her general character', Charlotte has brought to life the impression that she had of her mother many years later when first reading a bundle of her mother's letters to her father, discovering a 'mind of a truly fine, pure and elevated order.'*

However much you may dislike me now, I am sure you once loved me with an unaffected innocent love, and I feel confident that after all which you have seen and heard, you cannot doubt my love for you. It is now almost fifteen years since I last saw you. This is a long interval and may have effected many changes. It has made me look something older. But, I trust I have gained more than I have lost, I hope I may venture to say I am *wiser* and better … I cannot tell how *you* may feel on reading this, but I must say *my* ancient love is rekindled, and I have a *longing* desire to see you … And *whatever* you resolve upon, believe me to be yours *Most Sincerely* …

But Miss Burder was outraged:

> You have thought proper after a lapse of fifteen years and after various changes in circumstances again to address me, with what motives I cannot well define. The subject you have introduced so long ago buried in silence and until now almost forgotten cannot I should think produce in your mind anything like satisfactory reflection.

Patrick pressed home his claim that he had:

> Not the least doubt that if you had *been mine* you would have been happier than you *now* are or can be as one in *single* life. You would have had a *second self* … whose great aim would have been to have promoted your happiness in *both* worlds.

But it was to no avail; Miss Burder was unmoved by the prospect, and Patrick Brontë made no more romantic sallies. His dead wife's sister, Elizabeth, an upright,

LEFT *A miniature of Elizabeth Firth by an unknown artist. Miss Firth had welcomed the Brontë family to Thornton, and became Charlotte's godmother and a friend of the family. Despite her rejection of Patrick's proposal of marriage after Maria's death, he retained a very high opinion of her, proclaiming in 1836 that he would 'esteem it a high privilege' for Charlotte and Anne 'to be under your roof for a time, where, I am sure, they will see and hear nothing but what, under Providence, must necessarily attend to their best interests in both the worlds'.*

LEFT *A silhouette of Elizabeth Branwell, Maria's sister, who cared for the Brontë children after their mother's death in 1821. She was a devout Wesleyan, reserved and conscientious in her responsibilities. It was she who later supported the girls' plan to set up their own school and paid for Charlotte and Emily to study in Brussels. Branwell considered her 'for twenty years as my mother' and when she died he lamented that he had 'lost the guide and director of all the happy days connected with my childhood'.*

BELOW *The moors, an ever-present background to the Brontës' lives. Charlotte wrote from Roe Head School: 'that wind ... sounding wildly, unremittingly from hour to hour ... with a rapid, gathering stormy swell, that wind I know is heard at this moment far away on the moors at Haworth. Branwell and Emily hear it and as it sweeps over our house down the churchyard and round the old church, they think perhaps of me and Anne ...'*

Wesleyan woman, whom the children addressed as Aunt Branwell, had somewhat reluctantly but dutifully settled into the Parsonage to care for the motherless brood. It was, wrote Mrs Gaskell:

A GREAT CHANGE for a woman considerably past forty to come [from Cornwall] and take up her abode in a place where neither flowers nor vegetables would flourish, and where a tree of even moderate dimensions might be hunted for far and wide; where the snow lay long and late on the moors, stretching bleakly and barely far up from the dwelling which henceforward was to be her home. She missed the small round of cheerful, social visiting, perpetually going on in a country town, she missed her friends she had known from childhood ... she disliked many of the customs of the place and particularly dreaded the cold damp arising from the flagstones in the passages and parlours of Haworth Parsonage.

Patrick retreated more and more into his study to read and prepare his sermons. Each morning, with near perfect accuracy, he fired the pistol he had acquired during his time at Hartshead, when Luddite attacks were threatening new machinery and old beliefs, across the graveyard to ricochet off the tower of the church. He also took to taking lonely walks, striding across the moors, where golden eagles could still sometimes be seen swooping and wheeling high above the hills, and slashing at the heather and brambles with his cane.

CHAPTER 2
TALES OF CHILDHOOD

FOR THE RECENTLY BEREAVED Reverend Patrick Brontë, who had an income of just under £200 per annum and six children under ten, it seemed clear that the school at Cowan Bridge near Kirby Lonsdale in Lancashire, some fifty miles from Haworth, which had been recently opened by the evangelical vicar the Reverend William Carus Wilson, for the 'daughters of poor clergy', was the answer to the problems of his daughters' education. The fees were £14 a year for board, lodging and education and the prospectus explained that:

> THE SYSTEM OF EDUCATION comprehends History, Geography, the Use of the Globes, Grammar, Writing and Arithmetic; all kinds of Needlework, and the nicer kinds of household-work, such as getting up fine linen, etc. If Accomplishments are required, an additional charge is made, for French, Music, or Drawing, of £3 a year each … Each pupil must bring with her, a Bible and Prayer Book, a Workbag, with necessary Sewing Implements, etc., Combs, Brushes, Pair of Pattens, Gloves, and the following Articles of Clothing, etc.

4 Day Shifts	4 Pair of White Cotton Stockings
3 Night do.	3 Pair of Black Worsted do.
3 Night Caps	1 Nankeen Spencer
2 Pair of Stays	4 Brown Holland Pinafores
2 Flannel Petticoats	2 White do.
3 White Upper Petticoats	1 Short Coloured Dressing Gown
1 Grey Stuff do.	2 Pair of Shoes
2 Pair of Pockets	

On 1 July 1824, a little under three years after their mother's death, the two oldest Brontë children, Maria and Elizabeth, arrived at Cowan Bridge, to be followed by Charlotte in August and Emily in November.

Entries in the school register record the children's lack of systematic education and the careers the girls were destined for, but furnish hardly a glimpse of their acute and particular intelligence:

MARIA BRONTË, 10, 1824 July 21st. Vaccinated Chicken pox, Scarlet Fever, H. Cough [these appear under a heading 'Diseases had']. Reads tolerably – Writes pretty well – Ciphers a little – Works very badly – Knows a little of Grammar, very little of Geography and History – Has made some progress in reading French but knows nothing of the language grammatically. [On opposite page, the word 'Governess'.]

Elizabeth Brontë, 9 (ditto). Vaccinated Scarlet fever, H. Cough. Reads little – Writes pretty well – Ciphers none – Works very badly – Knows nothing of Grammar, Geography, History or Accomplishments.

Charlotte Brontë, 8, 1824 Augst. 10th. Vaccinated H. Cough. Reads tolerably – Writes indifferently – Ciphers a little and works neatly – Knows nothing of Grammar, Geography, History or Accomplishments. Governess. Altogether clever of her age but knows nothing systematically.

Emily Brontë, 5¾, 1824 Novbr. 25th. H. Cough. Reads very prettily & Works a little … Governess.

Cowan Bridge was to be a tragic, embittering – and, for the two eldest sisters, fatal – experience, and one which Charlotte immortalized some twenty years later as Lowood in *Jane Eyre*. The cruelties of the Reverend Carus Wilson are embodied in those of the sanctimonious Mr Brocklehurst, whom the ten-year-old Jane Eyre perceives as 'a black pillar! such at least appeared to me, at first sight, the straight, narrow, sable-clad shape standing erect on the rug: the grim face at the top was like a carved mask, placed above the shaft by way of capital.' Since his pupils were likely to remain impoverished all their lives – indeed, many were orphans – the fearsome minister of Tunstall devised a harsh and spartan

ABOVE *Sketches by Charlotte annotate the pages of the Reverend J. Goldsmith's* A Grammar of General Geography for the Use of Schools and Young Persons *(1823).*

regime at the school to inculcate humility and Christian resignation in his young students. The Reverend Wilson's pious and morbid writing, in such publications as *The Children's Friend, First Tales* and *Youthful Memoir*, reveal his moral purpose, which Charlotte later ascribed to Mr Brocklehurst of Lowood School in *Jane Eyre*:

> YOU ARE AWARE THAT MY PLAN in bringing up these girls is not to accustom them to habits of luxury and indulgence, but to render them hardy, patient, self-denying … Oh, madam, when you put bread and cheese, instead of burnt porridge, into these children's mouths, you may indeed feed their vile bodies, but you little think how you starve their immortal souls.

Charlotte described the cruel routines of the school through the eyes of the orphan Jane Eyre:

> DURING JANUARY, FEBRUARY, AND PART OF MARCH, the deep snows, and after their melting, the almost impassable roads, prevented our stirring beyond the garden walls, except to go to church; but within these limits we had to pass an hour every day in the open air. Our clothing was insufficient to protect us from the severe cold: we had no boots, the snow got into our shoes and melted there; our ungloved hands became numbed and covered with chilblains, as were our feet. I remember well the distracting irritation I endured from this cause every evening, when my feet inflamed; and the torture of thrusting the swelled, raw, and stiff toes into my shoes in the morning.

Sundays were dreary days in that wintry season. We had to walk two miles to Brocklebridge Church, where our patron officiated. We set out cold, we arrived at church colder; during morning service we became almost paralysed. It was too far to return to dinner, and an allowance of cold meat and bread, in the same penurious proportion observed in our ordinary meals, was served round between the services.

At the close of the afternoon service we returned by an exposed and hilly road, where bitter winter wind, blowing over a range of snowy summits to the north, almost flayed the skin from our faces …

How we longed for the light and heat of a blazing fire when we got back! But, to the little ones at least, this was denied: each hearth in the school-room was immediately surrounded by a double row of great girls and behind them younger children crouched in groups, wrapping their starved arms in their pinafores.

The Brontë children had arrived at Cowan Bridge still suffering from the after-effects of measles and whooping cough. That spring a typhus epidemic raged through the school and many of the ill-nourished girls fell victim. Again, Charlotte described the horrors in *Jane Eyre*:

THAT FOREST-DELL, WHERE LOWOOD LAY, was the cradle of fog and fog-bred pestilence; which, quickening with the quickening spring, crept into the Orphan Asylum, breathed typhus through its crowded school-room and dormitory, and,

ABOVE *The sampler of Maria Brontë, who died of tuberculosis in May 1825, aged eleven. Ellen Nussey recalled that 'whenever she [Charlotte] was certain of being quite alone with a friend she would talk of her two dead sisters, Maria and Elizabeth. Her love for them was most intense … she described Maria as a little mother among the rest, superhuman in goodness and cleverness.'*

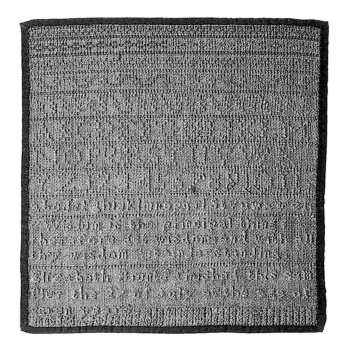

ABOVE *The sampler of Elizabeth Brontë, who died of tuberculosis in June 1825, aged ten. The childish fingers of the Brontë daughters would have stitched these samplers under the watchful eye of their mother and, after her death, their Aunt Branwell. Such work was regarded as educational, evidence of progress towards womanhood and housewifery, and it was common to embroider the alphabet and often a biblical text in fine silk on linen.*

ere May arrived, transformed the seminary into a hospital. Semi-starvation and neglected colds had predisposed most of the pupils to receive infection ... The teachers were fully occupied with packing up and making other necessary preparations for the departure of those girls who were fortunate enough to have friends and relations able and willing to remove them from the seat of contagion. Many, already smitten, went home only to die; some died at the school, and were buried quietly and quickly, the nature of the malady forbidding delay.

However, for Elizabeth, Charlotte and Emily, the typhus epidemic sweeping through Cowan Bridge School was a time of deliverance. Lessons were abandoned and, as for Jane Eyre, it was time of release and freedom:

> THEY LET US RAMBLE IN THE WOOD, like gipsies, from morning till night, we did what we liked, went where we liked; we lived better too ... our breakfast-basins were better filled; when there was no time to prepare a regular dinner, which often happened, [the housekeeper] would give us a large piece of cold pie, or a thick slice of bread and cheese, and this we carried away with us to the wood, where we each chose the spot we liked best, and dined sumptuously.

But Maria, who had been sent home in February with the wracking cough of tuberculosis, died there, in May, aged eleven. A fellow pupil described the school's callous neglect of Maria in graphic detail to Mrs Gaskell some thirty years later and she repeats the account in her biography:

THE DORMITORY IN WHICH MARIA SLEPT was a long room ... at one end ... there was a small bed-chamber ... appropriated to the use of Miss Scatcherd. Maria's bed stood nearest to the door of this room ... One morning, after she [Maria] had become so seriously unwell as to have to have a blister applied to her side (the sore from which was not perfectly healed), when the getting-up bell was heard, poor Maria moaned out that she was so ill, so very ill, she wished she might stop in bed; and some of the girls urged her to do so, and said they would explain it all to Miss Temple, the superintendent. But Miss Scatcherd was close at hand, and her anger would have to be faced before Miss Temple's kind thoughtfulness could interfere; so the sick child began to dress, shivering with cold, as, without leaving her bed, she slowly put on her black worsted stockings over her thin white legs (my informant spoke as if she saw it yet, and her whole face flashed out undying indignation). Just then, Miss Scatcherd issued from her room, and, without asking for a word of explanation from the sick and frightened girl, she took her by the arm, on the side to which the blister had been applied, and by one vigorous movement whirled her out into the middle of the floor, abusing her all the time for dirty and untidy habits. There she left her. My informant says Maria hardly spoke, except to beg some of the more indignant girls to be calm; but, in slow, trembling movements, with many a pause, she went downstairs at last – and was punished for being late.

BELOW *Lowood School. 'Miss Brontë ... said ... that she should not have written what she did of Lowood in "Jane Eyre", if she had thought the place would be so immediately identified with Cowan Bridge.'*

Charlotte created the saintly Helen Burns in *Jane Eyre* in memory of her sweet-natured, highly intelligent sister and substitute mother, Maria, whose death she was to mourn all her life; whilst Branwell, who had watched his sister's decline at the Parsonage, later wrote of her death and burial in his poem 'Caroline':

She lay with flowers about her head –
Though formal grave-clothes hid her hair!
Still did her lips the smile retain
Which parted them when hope was high,
Still seemed her brow as smoothed from pain
As when all thought she could not die …

They came – they pressed the coffin lid
Above my Caroline,
And then, I felt, for ever hid
My sister's face from mine!

ABOVE *The Reverend William Carus Wilson, a wealthy philanthropist and educator who was 'the prime mover in the establishment of this school [Cowan Bridge]' for the children of 'clergymen with limited incomes'.*

ABOVE RIGHT *A pencil sketch by Charlotte, said to be of Mr Brocklehurst, the headmaster of Lowood in* Jane Eyre, *who was the fictional double of the Reverend Carus Wilson of Cowan Bridge School.*

But another tragedy followed fast. Mrs Gaskell describes how:

THE NEWS OF [MARIA'S DEATH] … made those who remained at Cowan Bridge look with more anxiety on Elizabeth's symptoms, which also turned out to be consumptive. She was sent home … and she, too, died in the early summer of that year. Charlotte was thus suddenly called into the responsibilities of eldest sister to a motherless family. She remembered how anxiously her dear sister had striven in her grave, earnest way, to be a tender helper and a counsellor to them all; and the duties that now fell upon her seemed almost like a legacy from the gentle little sufferer so lately died.

Patrick Brontë, finally and urgently alerted to the dangers of Cowan Bridge, hastened to bring Charlotte and Emily home from 'that hateful place', and for the next five years, the four children lived and learned at home in an enclosed world bounded by the stone walls of the Parsonage, and enveloped in a universe of their own creation.

They were too poor to mix with the gentry but too educated to be at ease with the local farming families, who were 'a queer people' in Mrs Gaskell's somewhat biased view:

SMALL LANDED PROPRIETORS, dwelling in one spot since Q. Eliz – and lately adding marvellously to their incomes by using the water power of the peaks in the woollen manufacture which had sprung up during the last fifty years – uneducated – unrestrained by public opinion – for their equals in position are as bad as themselves … These people built grand houses, and live in the kitchens, own thousands of pounds and yet bring up their sons with only enough learning to qualify them for onlookers during their father's lifetime and greedy grasping money hunters after their father's death.

Yet in her opinion:

THE CHILDREN DID NOT WANT SOCIETY. To small infantine gaieties they were unaccustomed. They were all in all to each other. I do not suppose that there ever was a family more tenderly bound to one another … I suspect that they had no children's books and that their eager minds 'browzed undisturbed among the wholesome passages of English literature' … the servants of the household appeared to have been much impressed with the little Brontës' extraordinary cleverness.

The girls had lessons with Aunt Branwell in the room over the dining-room which she had taken for her own. Ellen Nussey, Charlotte's friend, described her:

ABOVE *A teapot believed to have belonged to Aunt Branwell. On the other side is the legend 'To Me/ To live is Chrift/To die is Gain', the favourite text of the celebrated preacher William Grimshaw, who preceded Patrick Brontë at Haworth. It is also inscribed over the door of the Methodist chapel Grimshaw built in West Lane.*

OPPOSITE *Charlotte Brontë's rosewood workbox. In her stuffy, overheated room Aunt Branwell 'made her nieces sew, with purpose or without', and when she died in 1842 Miss Branwell directed in her will, 'my Indian workbox I leave to my niece, Charlotte Brontë, my workbox with a china top I leave to my niece Emily Jane Brontë,' passing on through the female line a heritage of stitching and hemming, turning and patching, making and mending. Charlotte, who did not particularly like sewing, also kept three small pill boxes in her workbox, which probably contained palliatives for her frequent head- and toothaches.*

MISS BRANWELL WAS A VERY SMALL, antiquated little lady. She wore caps large enough for half a dozen of the present fashion, and a front of light auburn curls over her forehead. She always dressed in silk. She had a horror of the climate so far north, and of the stone floors in the parsonage. She amused us by clicking about in pattens whenever she had to go into the kitchen or look after household operations.

Aunt Branwell had moved into her bedroom, taken the youngest, Anne, to sleep with her, firmly shut and bolted the window, instructed the servants to bank up her fire against the Yorkshire damp, and rarely left her room. Indeed, she never ventured into the village, nor walked over the moors. Her only outing was when she crossed the churchyard every Sunday to sit in the front pew at St Michael and All Angels as part of the congregation to listen to her brother-in-law preach.

She took her meals on a tray in her room and it was to this overheated room that the three girls came for 'instructions in the household arts, in which Charlotte was afterwards such an adept'. Mary Taylor, whom Charlotte was to meet in 1831, recalls:

SHE MADE HER NIECES SEW, with purpose or without, and as far as possible discouraged any other culture. She used to keep the girls sewing charity clothing and maintained to me that it was not for the good of the recipients, but of the sewers. 'It was proper for them to do it,' she said.

But their education was not only in plain sewing. Whilst Patrick taught Branwell Greek and Latin and engaged a painting master for him, whenever he had the inclination, or could spare the time from his onerous parish duties, he would instruct his daughters in arithmetic or geography.

They joined in the painting lessons, and were later to be taught music. A piano was acquired, and although Charlotte was too short-sighted to play, Emily delighted in music. In addition, the children 'were always in the habit of picking up an immense amount of information for themselves'; there were books, for:

MR BRONTË ENCOURAGED A TASTE FOR READING in his girls; and though Miss Branwell kept it in due bounds, by the variety of household occupations, in which she expected them not merely to take a part, but become proficients, thereby

LEFT *A steel engraving from one of Sir Walter Scott's Waverley novels,* A Legend of Montrose *(1819). Charlotte greatly admired Scott's writing; as a girl she commended his 'sweet, wild, romantic poetry' to Ellen Nussey, and as a writer she was aware that her poems and novels, and those of Anne and, in particular, Emily, were much influenced by Scott's novels, with their concentration on themes of rural life and regional speech. However, in September 1848, she wrote to her publisher, 'were I obliged to copy any former novelist, even the greatest, even Scott, in anything, I would not write. Unless I have something of my own to say, and a way of my own to say it in, I have no business to publish.'*

occupying regularly a good portion of every day, they were allowed to get books from the circulating library at Keighley …

In 1834, Charlotte advised a friend on her reading:

IF YOU LIKE POETRY, LET IT BE FIRST RATE: Milton, Shakespeare, Thomson, Goldsmith, Pope (if you will, though I don't admire him), Scott, Byron, Campbell, Wordsworth, and Southey. Now, don't be startled at the names of Shakespeare and Byron. Both these were great men, and their works are like themselves … Omit the comedies of Shakespeare and the *Don Juan*, perhaps the *Cain*, of Byron, though the latter is a magnificent poem, and read the rest fearlessly – … Scott's sweet, wild, romantic poetry can do you no harm. Nor can Wordsworth's, nor Campbell's nor Southey's – the greatest part at least of his; some is certainly objectionable. For history, read Hume, Rollin, and the *Universal History*, if you can; I never did. For fiction, read Scott alone; all novels after his are worthless. For biography, read Johnson's *Lives of the Poets*, Boswell's *Life of Johnson*, Southey's *Life of Nelson*, Lockhart's *Life of Burns*, Moore's *Life of Sheridan*, Moore's *Life of Byron*, Wolfe's *Remains*. For natural history, read Bewick and Audubon, and Goldsmith and White's *History of Selborne*.

They were drawn into their father's concern with public affairs, which meant that he was:

IN THE HABIT of relating to them any public news in which he felt an interest; and from this strong and independent mind they would gather much food for thought.

Charlotte relates the excitement in April 1829:

WHEN THE INTELLIGENCE EXTRAORDINARY came with Mr Peel's speech in it containing the terms on which the Catholics were to be let in. With what eagerness papa tore off the cover and how we all gathered around him, and with what breathless anxiety we listened as one by one they were disclosed and explained and

ABOVE *Lord Byron (1788–1824), whose poetry infuses Charlotte's and Emily's work and their ideal of the heroic. Unlike many Victorian women, the Brontë daughters seem to have been allowed to read Byron's poetry – including* Don Juan *– and in 1833 their father purchased a copy of Byron's* Life and Works *edited by Moore.*

45

argued upon so ably and so well; and then, when it was all out, how aunt said she thought that it was excellent and that the Catholics [could] do no harm with such security. I remember also the doubts as to whether it would pass into the House of Lords and the prophecies that it would not. And when the paper came which was to describe the question, the anxiety was almost dreadful with which we listened to the whole affair: the opening of the doors, the hush, the Royal Dukes in their robes and the Great Duke in green sash and waistcoat, the rising of all the peeresses when he rose, the reading of his speech, papa saying that his words were like precious gold, and, lastly, the majority one to four in favour of the bill.

They benefited from the fact that their father subscribed to a considerable number of newspapers and periodicals, as Charlotte describes in her 'History of the Year 1829' when she was thirteen:

ONCE PAPA LENT MY SISTER MARIA A BOOK. It was an old geography-book; she wrote on its blank leaf, 'Papa lent me this book.' This book is a hundred and twenty years old; it is at this moment lying before me. While I write this I am in the kitchen of the Parsonage, Haworth; Tabby, the servant, is washing up the breakfast-things, and Anne, my youngest sister (Maria was my eldest), is kneeling on a chair, looking at some cakes which Tabby has been baking for us. Emily is in the parlour, brushing the carpet. Papa and Branwell are gone to Keighley. Aunt is upstairs in her room, and I am sitting by the table writing this in the kitchen. Keighley is a small town four miles from here. Papa and Branwell are gone for the newspaper, the *Leeds Intelligencer*, a most excellent Tory newspaper, edited by Mr. Wood, and the proprietor, Mr Henneman. We take two and see three newspapers a week. We take the *Leeds Intelligencer*, Tory, and the *Leeds Mercury*, Whig, edited by Mr Baines, and his brother, son-in-law, and his two sons ... We see the *John Bull*; it is a high Tory, very violent. Mr Driver lends us it, as likewise *Blackwood's Magazine*, the most able periodical there is.

OPPOSITE Woman Making Oatcakes, *from* The Costume of Yorkshire *by George Walker (1814). After their mother's death in 1821, a fifty-three-year-old Yorkshire woman, Tabitha Akroyd, came to the Parsonage as servant and cook, and, with the sometimes erratic help of Charlotte, Emily and Anne, prepared the plain fare which the Brontë family ate themselves, and, according to Ellen Nussey, sometimes passed on to their pets: 'There was ... but one dog that was admitted to the parlour at stated times. Emily and Anne always gave him a portion of their breakfast, which was, by their own choice, the old north country diet of oatmeal porridge.'*

And the Brontë children also grew up with the rich oral culture of Irish tales and north country folklore. There were the stories told by Tabitha Akroyd, who was, says Mrs Gaskell:

AN ELDERLY WOMAN OF THE VILLAGE [who] came to live as servant at the parsonage. She remained there, as a member of the household, for thirty years; and from the length of her faithful service, and the attachment and respect which she inspired, is deserving of mention. Tabby was a thorough specimen of a Yorkshire woman of her class, in dialect, in appearance, and in character. She abounded in strong practical sense and shrewdness. Her words were far from flattery; but she would spare no deeds in the cause of those whom she kindly regarded. She ruled the children pretty sharply; and yet never grudged a little extra trouble to provide them with such small treats as came within her power …

Tabby had lived in Haworth in the days when the pack-horses went through once a week, with their tinkling bells and gay worsted adornment, carrying the produce of the country from Keighley over the hills to Colne and Burnley. What is more, she had known the 'bottom', or valley, in those primitive days when the fairies frequented the margin of the 'beck' on moonlight nights, and had known folk who had seen them. But that was when there were no mills in the valleys; and when all the wool-spinning was done by hand in the farm-houses round. 'It wur the factories as had driven 'em away,' she said.

Although Patrick Brontë did not regularly converse with his children over dinner, since his dyspeptic disposition inclined him to take his meals alone in his study, he:

WOULD AT TIMES relate strange stories, which had been told to him by some of the oldest inhabitants of the parish, of the extraordinary lives and doings of people who had resided in far-off, out-of-the-way places, but in contiguity with

OPPOSITE *A pencil sketch, dated 4 March 1855, of St Simeon Stylites, one of the few of Emily Brontë's drawings to have survived. Like her sisters and brother, Emily carefully copied illustrations from books in the Parsonage. Charlotte writes about Lucy Snowe doing the same thing in* Villette: *'copying an elaborate line engraving, tediously working up my copy to the finish of the original, for that was my practical notion of art'. The choice of subject is interesting since Simeon Stylites was a monk of the early Christian Church who was noted for his extreme asceticism and piety, while Emily was the only one of the sisters who was exempted from teaching at Sunday school and who did not attend church regularly. Her poem 'No Coward Soul is Mine', written in 1846, seems her verdict on orthodox religion: 'Vain are the thousand creeds/That move men's hearts, unutterably vain,/Worthless as withered weeds/Or idlest froth amid the boundless main.'*

OPPOSITE *Sketches of various characters by Charlotte on the reverse of a pencil sketch of a cormorant sitting on a rock which she had copied from an engraving by Thomas Bewick in* A History of British Birds *(Volume II). This sketch is dated 24 January 1829, when Charlotte was thirteen. Three years later she penned some 'Lines on Bewick': '… And there 'mongst reeds upon a river's side/A wild bird sits, and brooding o'er her nest/Still guards the priceless gems, her joy and pride,/Now ripening 'neath her hope-enlivened breast.'*

Haworth – stories which made one shiver and shrink from hearing, but they were full of grim humour and interest to Mr Brontë and his children.

In addition, according to Mary Taylor, there was the pull of the moors, which were their playground:

THE THREE GIRLS used to walk upwards towards the 'purple black' moors, the sweeping surface of which was broken here and there by a stone quarry; and if they had the strength and time to go far enough, they reached a waterfall, where the beck fell over some rocks into the 'bottom'. They seldom went downwards through the village. They were shy of meeting even familiar faces, and were scrupulous about entering the house of the very poorest uninvited. They were steady teachers at the Sunday-school, a habit which Charlotte kept up very faithfully, even after she was left alone; but they never faced their kind voluntarily, and always preferred the solitude and freedom of the moors.

And then, as if to fuse all these solitary pleasures and preoccupations, there was 'making out'. Mary Taylor perceptively realized:

THIS HABIT OF 'MAKING OUT' interests for themselves that most children get who have none in actual life, was very strong in her [Charlotte]. The whole family used to 'make out' histories and invent characters and events. I told her sometimes they were like growing potatoes in a cellar. She said sadly, 'Yes! I know we are!'

But as Charlotte's poem 'Retrospection', written in 1835, shows, 'making out' this imaginary world gave the children a sense of freedom which she looked back on with envy when the realities of adult life intruded:

We wove a web in childhood,
A web of sunny air;
We dug a spring in infancy
Of water pure and fair;

We sowed in youth a mustard seed,
We cut an almond rod.
We are now grown to riper age;
Are they withered in the sod?

Are they blighted ,failed and faded,
Are they mouldered back to clay?
For life is darkly shaded
And its joys fleet fast away!

Charlotte sketched out how it had all begun:

PAPA BOUGHT BRANWELL SOME WOODEN SOLDIERS at Leeds; when Papa came home it was night, and we were in bed, so next morning Branwell came to our door with a box of soldiers. Emily and I jumped out of bed, and I snatched up one and exclaimed, 'This is the Duke of Wellington! This shall be the Duke!' When I had said this Emily likewise took up one and said it should be hers; when Anne came down, she said one should be hers. Mine was the prettiest of the whole, and the tallest, and the most perfect in every part. Emily's was a grave-looking fellow, and we called him 'Gravey'. Anne's was a queer little thing, much like herself, and we called him 'Waiting-Boy'. Branwell chose his, and called him 'Buonaparte'.

As she explained in her introduction to 'Tales of the Islanders', the world that the children spun for themselves took its landmarks and people from the wider world; refracted in books and periodicals, politics and happenings far away from their

LEFT *Dated 12 March 1827, this is one of the earliest books by the Brontë children to survive. Produced by Branwell when he was nine, its cover is made from a blue paper sugar bag, with four pages sewn together to form a book. It appears to have been planned as a story about Sneakey (Buonaparte), one of the twelve toy soldiers brought home by their father that 'founded' Glass Town, and who was later created king of an imaginary kingdom, Sneachiesland, in a mythical Africa. This page shows the 'Battell of W[a]shington' and a map of North and South America, and probably owes its inspiration to a series of illustrations about the British Army fighting in Washington and Orleans during the American War of 1812 which* had appeared in Blackwood's Magazine *that spring.*

own experiences at the Parsonage were as present to them as anything of their everyday life.

THE PLAY OF THE 'ISLANDERS' was formed in December 1827, in the following manner. One night, about the time when the cold sleet and stormy fogs of November are succeeded by the snow-storms and high piercing night-winds of confirmed winter, we were all sitting round the warm blazing kitchen fire, having just concluded a quarrel with Tabby concerning the propriety of lighting a candle, from which she came off victorious, no candle having been produced. A long pause succeeded, which was at last broken by Branwell saying, in a lazy manner, 'I don't know what to do.' This was echoed by Emily and Anne.

Tabby – 'Wha ya may go t'bed.'
Branwell – 'I'd rather do anything than that.'
Charlotte – 'Why are you so glum to-night, Tabby? Oh! suppose we had each an island of our own.'
Branwell – 'If we had I would choose the Island of Man.'
Charlotte – 'And I would choose the Isle of Wight.'
Emily – 'The Isle of Arran for me.'
Anne – 'And mine should be Guernsey.'

We then chose who should be chief men in our islands. Branwell chose John Bull, Astley Cooper, and Leigh Hunt; Emily, Walter Scott, Mr Lockhart, Johnny Lockhart; Anne, Michael Sadler, Lord Bentinck, Sir Henry Halford. I chose the Duke of Wellington and two sons, Christopher North and Co., and Mr Abernethy. Here our conversation was interrupted by the, to us, dismal sound of the clock striking seven, and we were summoned off to bed. The next day we added many others to our list of men, till we got almost all the chief men of the

ABOVE *The Duke of Zamorna, drawn by Branwell, c.1831. This imaginary character started life as Arthur Augustus Adrian Wellesley, Marquis of Douro (named after the son and heir of the Duke of Wellington), and later became King and then Emperor of Angria, the kingdom east of Glass Town.*

ABOVE *The Duke of Wellington, hero of the Peninsular Campaign and Waterloo, and Tory Prime Minister (1828–30). He was the particular hero of Charlotte Brontë who made him the central character, in various manifestations, in her stories of Glass Town and Angria.*

ABOVE *Arthur Augustus Adrian Wellesley, drawn by Charlotte, who metamorphoses into the Duke of Zamorna, the King of Angria and, eventually, the Emperor Adrian. Here, as a young man, he has a 'mild and human disposition', but as Zamorna 'his wild blood boils from his heart.'*

ABOVE *'English Lady', a detailed pencil copy of W. H. Finden's engraving of the portrait of Lady Jersey which Charlotte would have seen in Moore's* Life Of Byron. *She has deliberately changed minor details so that the drawing could serve as a portrait of an Angrian heroine.*

kingdom. After this, for a long time, nothing worth noticing occurred. In June 1828, we erected a school on a fictitious island, which was to contain 1,000 children. The manner of the building was as follows. The island was fifty miles in circumference, and certainly appeared more like the work of enchantment than anything real, &c.

These characters, many based on the Napoleonic Wars, which had raged across Europe so recently, peopled the Brontë children's 'world below' as Charlotte called it, with the 'Young Men' (or 'The Twelves', as they came to be called) becoming part of a saga of epic adventures, wars, politics, love and intrigue. Each had her or his own kingdom – Wellington's Land (after the duke) was Charlotte's, Parry's Land was Emily's, and Ross's Land, Anne's (both called after the Arctic explorers), while Branwell ruled over Sneakey's Land. Branwell mapped and conflated the kingdom into a whole world, 'The Great Glass Town Confederacy', later renamed with a classical flourish Verdopolis, which had glorious vistas and abundance conjured up in the quiet, simple rooms of the Parsonage:

> ITS STATELY TOWERS AND TURRETS shone like fairy buildings of gold. Ships crowded the distant harbour. Magnificent barges and yachts were skimming with spread sails over its deep blue bosom, while the oar-chant of the rowers and the louder voice of commerce came with such distinctness through the calm, clear atmosphere that the words they offered may have been heard by an attentive listener.

It also possessed all the agencies of the real world, with heroes and generals, artists and villains, inns, publishers, writers and magazines. All the lands were presided over by the four Genii

LEFT *Belshazzar's Feast by John Martin (1789–1854). A mezzotint of this apocalyptic painting hung in the Parsonage at Haworth. The Brontë children internalized the painting's drama and visionary power and created Angria and Gondal as the written equivalent to its visual magnificence; the geometric Babylonian grandeur also inspired the architecture of Glass Town. The Old Testament Story depicted by the painting was later to colour Charlotte's description of the ideal critic to understand Emily's book* Wuthering Heights: *one who could interpret 'the writing on the wall ... who can accurately read the "Mene, Tekel, Upharsin" of an original mind'.*

– by which device the children wove themselves into their make-believe world – Tallii (Charlotte), Branii, Emmii and Annii. The Genii had omnipotent powers and could resurrect the dead, a wishful fantasy created soon after the deaths of their two older sisters.

The Brontës were already writers; experimenting with voice and form, and so their characters had to have a chronicle for their kingdom. In their mass of childhood outpourings, the prentice work of writers, there are more words than in their entire published works. *The Young Man's Magazine* was modelled on *Blackwood's Magazine*; it was toy-soldier size, about 2½ by 1¼ inches, stitched into sugar-paper covers which had been wheedled out of Tabby. They were written in a tiny, spidery hand, designed to look like print and confound all but the youngest, sharpest eyes. To Mrs Gaskell, these miniature tracts were 'an immense amount of manuscript in an inconceivably small space'.

First written by Branwell and filled with tales of battles, civil wars and conquest, the writing was soon appropriated by Charlotte:

*ALL SOBERNESS is past and gone
the reign of gravity is done
Frivolity comes in its place
light smiling sits on every face.*

*Gone is that grave and gorgeous light
which every page illumined bright
a flimsy torch glare in their stead
of a bright golden sun now fled.*

*Foolish romances now employ
each silly senseless girl and boy
O for the strong hand of the law
to stop it with its powerful claw.*

And, by conquest, she acquired a new kingdom of Angria, based on a mythic Africa exotic with tropical flora and Palladian palaces; she awarded its rule to one of the sons of the Duke of Wellington, Arthur Wellesley, Marquis of Douro, and created him Duke of Zamorna and King of Angria. Zamorna was a Byronic aristocrat who was soon supplied with two wives, a panoply of mistresses and a permanent feud with Branwell's creation, Northangerland, giving Charlotte rich opportunities to spin stories of intrigue and deceit, love and passion.

In turn, Emily and Anne seceded from Angria and brought into being the land of Gondal, an island in the Pacific which nevertheless had a climate strangely like Haworth, and a Queen, Augusta Geraldine Almeda, who was wild and wilful and ruled over a passionate people. The melodrama of Gondal was woven into the fabric of Emily's existence and it stayed with her all her life: many of her poems take their themes from the Gondal Chronicles. On 30 July 1845, she wrote in the diary paper she and Anne recorded every four years:

> MY BIRTHDAY – showery, breezy, cool. I am twenty-seven years old today … Anne and I went for our first long journey by ourselves together, leaving home on the 30th June, Monday sleeping at York, returning to Keighley Tuesday evening, sleeping there and walking home on Wednesday morning. Though the weather was very broken we enjoyed ourselves very much, except during a few hours at Bradford. And during our excursion we were, Ronald

BELOW *The* Monthly Intelligencer, *a miniature facsimile newspaper produced by Branwell between 27 March and 26 April 1833. The Brontës were avid newspaper-readers; Patrick took the* Leeds Intelligencer, *the* Leeds Mercury *and* John Bull *and the children followed all the political news. Like the miniature magazines Branwell had produced before, modelled on Blackwood's, this replica newspaper was of a size and content appropriate to the 'Young Men', the toy soldiers, with news of the sessions of the Great Glass Town Parliament and a poem by Young Soult, all laid out in a proper newspaper format.*

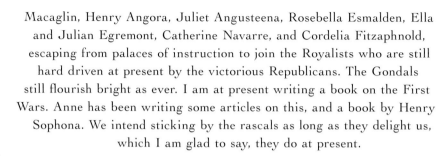

CONTENTS

ST FOR AU
1830

1830
CHARLOTTE
BRONTE

BELOW AND RIGHT *By 1829 the Brontë children were writing and producing a series of miniature books to chronicle the Lilliputian world of Glass Town (to become Verdopolis). Mrs Gaskell described them as 'an immense amount of manuscript, in an inconceivably small space; tales, dramas, poems, romances, written principally by Charlotte, in a hand which it is almost impossible to decipher without the aid of a magnifying glass'.*

Macaglin, Henry Angora, Juliet Angusteena, Rosebella Esmalden, Ella and Julian Egremont, Catherine Navarre, and Cordelia Fitzaphnold, escaping from palaces of instruction to join the Royalists who are still hard driven at present by the victorious Republicans. The Gondals still flourish bright as ever. I am at present writing a book on the First Wars. Anne has been writing some articles on this, and a book by Henry Sophona. We intend sticking by the rascals as long as they delight us, which I am glad to say, they do at present.

And whilst Charlotte put childish things behind her and bade her farewells to Angria when she set off for school again in January 1831, aged fifteen, she took up the Angria stories on her return eighteen months later. It was not until she was twenty-three that Charlotte finally left the world of Zamorna and Northangerland, Rogue, the wicked pirate, and Mina Laury, the temptress, behind; and even then she was reluctant to abandon the 'web of sunny air' which she and her siblings had spun:

YET DO NOT URGE ME too fast, reader: it is no easy theme to dismiss from my imagination the images that have filled it so long. They were my friends and my intimate acquaintances, and I could with little labour describe to you the faces, the voices, the actions, of those who people my thoughts by day, and not seldom stole strangely even into my dreams by night. When I depart from these I feel almost as if I stood on the threshold of a home and were bidding farewell to its inmates … Still, I long to quit for a while that burning clime where we have sojourned too long – its skies flame, the glow of sunset is always upon it. The mind would cease from excitement and turn now to a cooler region where the dawn breaks grey and sober, and the coming day for a time at least is subdued by clouds.

CHAPTER 3
A SUITABLE SITUATION

'YOU EVIDENTLY POSSESS, and in no inconsiderable degree, what Wordsworth calls "the faculty of verse",' wrote the poet laureate, Robert Southey to Charlotte Brontë, who had written twenty-two 'volumes' of juvenilia by the time she was fourteen, and had shyly sent him a number of her poems at Christmas 1836. But, he continues:

> LITERATURE CANNOT BE the business of a woman's life, and it ought not to be. The more she is engaged in her proper duties, the less leisure she will have for it, even as an accomplishment and a recreation. To those duties you have not been called, and when you are you will be less eager for celebrity. You will not seek in imagination for excitement …

The 'duty' which the venerable poet seemed to envisage was that of being a wife. But Charlotte, Emily and Anne Brontë could not depend on that eventuality. Their circumstances meant that they had to reckon on the necessity of earning their own living.

Their father had been very ill in the spring of 1831, and feared that he would 'never fully recover. I sometimes think that I shall fall into a decline.' He did not; despite his nervous digestion, his myopia and his fear of bronchitis, which caused him to encircle his throat in ever-rising layers of silk to ward off the cold, he outlasted his family by many years, dying in 1861 at the age of eighty-four.

But his illness raised the terrible spectre of destitution. What would happen to the four Brontë children, the oldest of whom, Charlotte, was then only sixteen, were they to be left orphans? A clergyman lives in the equivalent of a tied cottage. In the event of their father's death, there would be no home, and no money, for Mr Brontë would have been unable to save out of his meagre stipend, and Aunt Branwell's £50 annuity could hardly keep a family of five.

OPPOSITE The Governess *by Richard Redgrave, 1844, a poignant representation of the plight of the genteel governess, as alone, unregarded, she sits in shadow whilst her pupils, the daughters of the house, take their pleasures in the light. The music on the piano is 'Home, Sweet Home'. Charlotte, Emily and Anne all keenly experienced the privations and humiliations of teaching. Charlotte wrote to Emily when she went as a governess to the Sidgwick family in 1839: 'I see now more clearly than I have ever done before that a private governess has no existence, is not considered as a living and rational being except as connected with the wearisome duties she has to fulfil.'*

The children had to contemplate making their own way in the world. They would have to be trained for a career. For the only son, Branwell, the prospects seemed bright. He was seen as the talented one in the family; the painting master his father had engaged was regarded as an investment, whilst Branwell himself also contemplated the life of a writer – a great poet, perhaps, or a contributor to periodicals such as *Blackwood's Magazine*, following in the footsteps of luminaries like James Hogg. For the girls the options were severely limited.

The 'duty' to which the three Brontë sisters would all be called was that of governess – which in the mid-nineteenth century meant someone who either taught in a school, or, more usually, lived in her employer's house, taught the children and served as a companion to them. In 1851 there were about 25,000 governesses in England; they were usually genteel, educated – and poor. Thus it was considered an entirely suitable occupation for the daughters of the clergy. But it was often not a happy one since, as Lady Eastlake wrote:

> THE REAL DEFINITION of a governess in the English sense is a being who is our equal in birth, manners and education, but our inferior in worldly wealth.

In January 1831 Charlotte set off for school for the second time in her life, leaving behind at the Parsonage her brother and sisters in their 'world within' of imagination and relative freedom, to acquire the formal and systematic education which would, it was hoped, qualify her to find a position.

The school was Roe Head near Dewsbury in Yorkshire, some twenty miles from Haworth, and Charlotte's fees there were paid by her godmother, Frances Atkinson, and her husband. It was run by the Misses Wooler, the oldest of whom, Margaret, was headmistress to the ten or so pupils who boarded at the school. Miss Wooler was 'short and stout, but graceful in her movements, very fluent in conversation, and with a sweet voice'. She habitually dressed in white, like an abbess, her hair braided in coils around her head, and possessed a considerable

OPPOSITE *Roe Head School, Mirfield, a pencil sketch by Anne Brontë, who, in her first departure from the Parsonage, in October 1835, replaced Emily at the Misses Wooler's school, where Charlotte had returned as a teacher. A poem she wrote the following autumn is witness to her resolution for her new life: 'But the world's before me now,/Why should I despair?/I will not spend my days in vain,/I will not linger here!/I will leave thee then my childhood's home,/For all thy joys are gone,/I leave thee through the world to roam/In search of fair renown.'*

intellect. She was to become a firm friend to Charlotte in later years and show her much kindness.

Mary Taylor, one of her fellow pupils, observed Charlotte's arrival from the window:

I FIRST SAW HER coming in a covered cart in very old-fashioned clothes, and looking very cold and miserable. She was coming to school at Miss Wooler's. When she appeared in the schoolroom her dress was changed, but just as old. She looked a little, old woman, so short-sighted that she always appeared to be seeking something, and moving her head from side to side to catch a sight of it. She was very shy and nervous, and spoke with a strong Irish accent. When a book was given her she dropped her head over it till her nose nearly touched it, and when she was told to hold her head up, up went the book after it, still close to her nose, so that it was not possible to help laughing.

We thought her very ignorant, for she had never learnt grammar at all, and very little geography.

She would confound us by knowing things that were out of our range altogether. She was acquainted with most of the short pieces of poetry that we had to learn by heart: would tell us the authors, the poems they were taken from, and sometimes repeat a page or two, and tell us the plot. She had a habit of writing in italics (printing characters), and said she had learnt it by writing in their magazine. They brought out a 'magazine' once a month, and wished it to look as like print as possible. She told us a tale out of it. 'No one wrote in it, and

ABOVE *When she first went out into the world of school and governessing, Charlotte drew comfort from 'making out', retreating into the imaginary world of her childhood, but she began to realize – with a sense of loss – that she would have to leave this 'world within' (of which this miniature book was a part). In January 1841 she wrote: 'Once … I was very poetical … but I am now …. approaching twenty-five … At this age it is time that the imagination should be pruned and trimmed … and a few at least, of the countless illusions of early youth should be cleared away.'*

ABOVE The Carrier's Cart in Summer, *by William Francis Freelove, the leitmotif of the Brontë children's life between 1851 and 1845 as at various times each one of them would pack a box with their possessions, put it on the cart and set out for a new school, a new position, a new life, only to return to the Parsonage weeks or months later, bruised and chastened by their forays into the outside world, to be soothed by the unchanging, restricted life of the Parsonage before they made the next assault.*

no one read it, but herself, her brother, and two sisters. She promised to show me some of these magazines, but retracted it afterwards, and would never be persuaded to do so. In our play hours she sat or stood still, with a book, if possible. Some of us once urged her to be on our side in a game at ball. She said she had never played, and could not play. We made her try, but soon found that she could not see the ball, so we put her out. She took all our proceedings with pliable indifference, and always seemed to need a previous resolution to say 'No' to anything. She used to go and stand under the trees in the playground, and say it was pleasanter. She endeavoured to explain this, pointing out the shadows, the peeps of sky, etc. We understood but little of it.

It was at Roe Head that Charlotte was to make the first real friends any of the children had outside their own family circle. Mary Taylor and her sister Martha were to become close, if sometimes critical and outspoken, companions. They were the daughters of a political radical, a former prosperous cloth manufacturer whose business had been ruined when the demand for uniforms dried up at the end of the Napoleonic wars. Charlotte was to use Mary as a model for Rose York in *Shirley*, characterizing her as '[a girl] who believed that it was better to try all things and find all empty, than to try nothing and leave your life a blank.'

Charlotte visited the family several times at the distinctive Red House at Gomersal, where they lived, and, in later years, recalled that 'the society of the Taylors is one of the most rousing pleasures I have ever known.'

Her other new friend was Ellen Nussey, a complete contrast to the determined Mary Taylor and her sister Martha, tagged 'little Miss Boisterous', at Roe Head. Ellen was the youngest of twelve children and lived with her recently widowed mother at Rydings, a large old turreted house some ten miles from the school, which Branwell was to pronounce as 'paradise' when he visited there. Although her father's recent death had meant that the Nusseys' immediate circumstances were somewhat straitened, the family had 'old money', in contrast to the new wealth of the Yorkshire manufacturers, and were a respected 'county' family of Conservative persuasion. Charlotte recognized her need for both companions in a letter she wrote to Ellen:

> I HAVE TWO STUDIES. You are my study for the success, the credit and the responsibility of a quiet tranquil character; Mary is my study for remorse, the misconstruction which follow the development of feelings in themselves noble, warm, generous, devoted and profound, but which, being too fully revealed, too fully bestowed, are not estimated at their real value. I never hope to see in this world a character more truly noble. She would die willingly for one she loved. Her intellect and attainments are of the very highest standard. Yet I doubt whether Mary will ever marry.

Mary did not marry. She emigrated to New Zealand where she eventually ran a shop single-handed before returning to England in 1860 and wrote articles and a novel, *Miss Miles*, arguing for women's need for independence, thus fully justifying Charlotte's verdict:

> MARY ALONE HAS MORE power in her nature than any ten men you can pick out in the united parishes of Birstall and Haworth. It is vain to limit a character like hers within ordinary boundaries. She will overstep them. I am morally certain that Mary will establish her own landmarks.

The 'quiet tranquil' Ellen Nussey was to establish no landmarks, but was to remain Charlotte's friend for the rest of her life; and their letters, which span nearly

ABOVE *A drawing by Charlotte of Ellen Nussey as a schoolgirl. Charlotte wrote to thank her for a gift in 1834: 'the bonnet is pretty, neat and simple, as like the giver as possible. It brought Ellen Nussey with her fair, quiet face, brown eyes and dark hair full to my remembrance.'*

RIGHT *'Miss W[ooler] had two badges of conduct for her pupils which were wonderfully effective, except for the most careless. A black ribbon, worn in the style of the Order of the Garter, which the pupils passed from One to another for any breach of rules, unlady-like manners, or incorrect grammar. Charlotte may, in her very earliest school-days, have worn "the mark" as we styled it, but I never remember her having it,' wrote Ellen Nussey. 'The silver medal [shown here], which was the badge for the fulfilment of duties, she won the right to in her first half-year. This she never again forfeited, and it was presented to her on leaving school.'*

twenty-five years, provide our most authentic testimony to the life of the Brontës.

When Charlotte was away at school, her closest companion and fellow in bedtime stories, Emily, drew nearer to her younger sister. Soon Anne and Emily were inseparable in life and in league over their new kingdom, Gondal. To some extent, perhaps, her new friend assuaged that loss, but Charlotte recognized that the docile, commonsensical, somewhat pedestrian Ellen had her limitations:

> **WHEN I FIRST SAW** Ellen I did not care for her; we were school fellows ...
> We were contrasts ... still we suited ... She is without romance. If she attempts to
> read poetry, or poetic prose aloud, I am irritated and deprive her of the book ... but
> she is good; she is true, she is faithful, and I love her ...

If Ellen provided Charlotte with the accepting stability of the unimaginative which was sometimes able to reassure her fears and depressions, Charlotte kept from her friend the wilder shores of her own imaginings. She never told Ellen about 'making out', the world of Angria grew, unconfessed, as did her identity of the author of *Jane Eyre* when it was published.

Despite her supposed lack of education when she arrived at Roe Head, Charlotte was soon recognized as the star pupil. 'She was only three half-years at school,' Ellen Nussey explained, '[but] In this time she went through all the elementary teaching contained in our school books. She was in the habit of committing long pieces of poetry to memory, and seemed to do so with real enjoyment and hardly any effort.'

Charlotte returned to the Parsonage in the early summer of 1832, and the children were in a state of grace for three more years. Charlotte wrote of this time to Ellen:

> YOU ASK ME to give you a description of the manner in which I have passed every day since I left School: this is soon done, as an account of one day is an account of all. In the morning from nine o'clock till half past twelve, I instruct my Sisters and draw, then we walk till dinner, after dinner I sew till tea time, and after tea I either read, write, do a little fancy work or draw, as I please. Thus in one delightful though somewhat monotonous course my life is passed.

In the summer of 1833, Ellen paid her first visit to the Parsonage (Charlotte had been a guest at Rydings the previous January) and gave her impressions of the household:

> 'TABBY', THE FAITHFUL, TRUSTWORTHY OLD SERVANT, was very quaint in appearance – very active, and, in these days, the general servant and factotum. We were all 'childer' and 'bairns', in her estimation. She still kept to her duty of walking out with the 'childer', if they went any distance from home, unless Branwell were sent by his father as a protector …

> Emily Brontë had by this time acquired a lithesome, graceful figure. She was the tallest person in the house, except her father. Her hair, which was naturally as beautiful as Charlotte's, was in the same unbecoming tight curl and frizz, and there was the same want of complexion. She had very beautiful eyes – kind, kindling,

OPPOSITE *An untitled watercolour by Charlotte Brontë, its provenance verified by her father. According to Branwell's friend and biographer, F. A. Leyland, the young Charlotte 'even thought of art as a profession for herself; and so strong was this intention, that she should scarcely be convinced that it was not her true vocation. But although she had occasional lessons from the Leeds artist William Robinson, by 1848, when she was in her thirties, Charlotte rejected a suggestion from her publisher that she might like to illustrate* Jane Eyre *herself, 'because I have not the skill you attribute to me … It is not enough to have the artist's eye, one must also have the artist's hand to turn the first gift to practical account.'*

By my daughter Charlotte,
L Brontë, Ms

liquid eyes; but she did not often look at you: she was too reserved. Their colour might be said to be dark grey, at other times dark blue, they varied so. She talked very little. She and Anne were like twins – inseparable companions, and in the very closest sympathy, which never had any interruption.

Anne – dear, gentle Anne – was quite different in appearance from the others. She was her aunt's favourite. Her hair was a very pretty, light brown, and fell on her neck in graceful curls. She had lovely violet-blue eyes, fine pencilled eyebrows, and clear, almost transparent complexion. She still pursued her studies, and especially her sewing, under the surveillance of her aunt. Emily had now begun to have the disposal of her own time.

Branwell studied regularly with his father, and used to paint in oils, which was regarded as study for what might be eventually his profession. All the household entertained the idea of his becoming an artist, and hoped he would be a distinguished one.

In fine and suitable weather delightful rambles were made over the moors, and down into the glens and ravines that here and there broke the monotony of the moorland. The rugged bank and rippling brook were treasures of delight. Emily, Anne, and Branwell used to ford the streams, and sometimes placed stepping-stones for the other two; there was always a lingering delight in these spots – every moss, every flower, every tint and form, were noted and enjoyed. Emily especially had a gleesome delight in these nooks of beauty – her reserve for the time vanished.

But things at the Parsonage had changed almost imperceptibly. Roe Head had brought Charlotte friends and a small degree of social confidence. It had certainly given

RIGHT *'In fine and suitable weather delightful rambles were made over the moors, and down into the glens and ravines that here and there broke the monotony of the moorland', recalls Ellen Nussey of a visit she paid to Haworth in 1833. 'One long ramble made in these early days was far away over the moors to see a spot familiar to Emily and Anne which they called "The Meeting of the Waters" … Emily, half reclining on a slab of stone, played like a young child with the tadpoles in the water, making them swim about, and then fell to moralizing on the strong and the weak, the brave and the cowardly as she chased them with her hand. No serious care or sorrow had so far cast its gloom on nature's youth and buoyancy, and nature's simplest offerings were fountains of pleasure and enjoyment.'*

ABOVE *The first diary paper of Emily and Anne. This is the only joint paper; subsequently, the sisters wrote separate ones and exchanged and read them four years later.*

her an awareness of the possibilities of the wider world. Henceforth it was to be Charlotte who was more anxious than her sisters to explore the 'world without', though at considerable emotional cost.

For Emily, however, the Parsonage provided a seamless universe where the quotidian merged with the imaginary and fantastic, and every subsequent attempt to detach her from this world was to end in failure. The entry for 'November 24th 1834, Monday' in the diary paper which Anne and Emily signed jointly every four years as a marker to their quiet lives speaks of Emily's preoccupations and is evidence of her chaotic spelling and grammar.

I FED RAINBOW, Diamond, Snowflake, Jasper pheasant (alias). This morning Branwell went down to Mr Driver's and brought news that Sir Robert Peel was going to be invited to stand for Leeds. Anne and I have been peeling apples for Charlotte to make an apple pudding and for Aunt's … Charlotte said she made puddings perfectly and she … of a quick but lim[i]ted intellect. Taby said just now Come Anne pilloputate (i.e. pill [peel] a potato) Aunt has come into the kitchin just now and said Where are your feet Anne Anne answered On the floor Aunt. Papa opened the parlour door and gave Branwell a letter saying Here Branwell read this and show it to your Aunt and Charlotte. The Gondals are discovering the interior of Gaaldine. Sally Mosley is washing in the back kitchin.

It is past twelve o'clock Anne and I have not tid[i]ed ourselves, done our bed work, or done our lessons and we want to go out to play. We are going to have for dinner Boiled Beef, Turnips, potatoes and apple pudding. The kitchin is in a very untidy state Anne and I have not done our music exercise which consists of *b major* Taby said on my putting a pen in her face Ya pitter pottering there instead of pilling a potate. I answered O Dear, O Dear, O Dear I will derectly With that I get up, take a knife and begin pilling. Finished pilling the potatoes Papa going to walk Mr Sunderland expected.

Anne and I say I wonder what we shall be like and what we shall be and where we shall be, if all goes on well, in the year 1874 – in which year I shall be in my 57th year. Anne will be in her 55th year Branwell will be going in his 58th year and Charlotte in her 59th year Hoping we shall all be well at that time We close our paper.

But all this had to change. Charlotte wrote to Ellen in July 1835:

> WE ARE ALL ABOUT TO DIVIDE, break up, separate, Emily is going to school, Branwell is going to London, and I am going to be a Governess. This last determination I formed myself, knowing that I should have to take the step sometime, and 'better sune as syne' to use the Scotch proverb and knowing also that Papa would have enough to do with his limited income should Branwell be placed at the Royal Academy, and Emily at Roe Head. Where am I going to reside? you will ask – within four miles of yourself dearest at a place neither of us are wholly unacquainted with, being no other than Roe Head … Yes I am going to teach in the very school where I was myself taught – Miss Wooler made me the offer and I preferred it to one or two proposals of Private Governess-ship which I had before received – I am sad, very sad at the thoughts of leaving home but Duty – Necessity … these are stern mistresses who will not be disobeyed. Did I not once say Ellen you ought to be thankful for your independence?

Branwell was now eighteen and it was time that he sought to make his way in the world. Calling him Patrick Benjamin Wiggins, Charlotte caricatured her brother that autumn with an affectionate portrait in 'My Angria and the Angrians':

ABOVE *Self-portrait by Branwell Brontë. In 1835 Branwell, who had been taking art lessons and also cajoling the editor of* Blackwood's Magazine *to use his work ('I know that I possess strength to assist you beyond your own contributors'), took the decision to enter as a probationary student in the Royal Academy.*

ABOVE *A fragment from the so-called 'gun group' portrait, painted by Branwell, of Emily Brontë. It was torn out by Charlotte's husband, the Reverend Arthur Bell Nicholls, who, unhappy with the likeness of his wife, destroyed the rest of the picture.*

RIGHT *Branwell did not present himself at the Royal Academy Schools as planned, but wandered the streets of London 'with a wildest dejected look', spending his money in the Castle Inn, Holborn, drinking 'little squibs of rum'. He returned to Haworth claiming to have been tricked out of his funds.*

[HE WAS] A LOW SLIGHTLY BUILT MAN attired in a black coat and raven grey trousers, his hat placed nearly at the back of his head, revealing a bush of carroty hair so arranged that at the sides it projected almost like two spread hands, a pair of spectacles placed across a prominent Roman nose, black neckerchief adjusted with no attention to precision, and to complete the picture, a little black rattan flourished in his hand. His bearing as he walked was tolerably upright and marked with that indescribable swing always assumed by those who pride themselves on being good pedestrians.

Branwell was to go to London and enter the Royal Academy Schools to train as an artist whilst Charlotte was to take Miss Wooler's offer that she should return to Roe Head as a teacher. Emily could attend as a pupil with her fees paid out of her older sister's earnings – a marvellous opportunity it seemed for Emily, who, when painstakingly stitching the samplers her aunt required her to busy her fingers with, still managed to get the letters of the alphabet out of sequence.

None of these ventures was a success. Branwell was exposed – and succumbed – to temptation, with the result that his sojourn in London lasted less than a

fortnight. He failed to present himself at the Academy, and returned home having, it appeared, spent the money Aunt Branwell had saved to set her favourite on the path to artistic achievement, on drink and low life in the taverns of the capital.

Emily lasted only three months at Roe Head. She would speak to no one except

Charlotte, would not eat, and grew thin and pale. Charlotte understood the reason:

MY SISTER EMILY loved the moors. Flowers brighter than the rose bloomed in the blackest of the heath for her – out of a sullen hollow in a livid hill-side, her mind could make an Eden. She found in the bleak solitude many and dear delights; and not the least and best-loved was liberty. Liberty was the breath of Emily's nostrils; without it she perished. The changes from her own home to a school and from her own very noiseless, very secluded, but unrestricted and unartificial mode of life, to one of disciplined routine (though under the kindest auspices), was what she failed in enduring. Her nature proved here too strong for her fortitude. Every morning when she woke, the vision of home and the moors rushed on her, and darkened and saddened the day that lay before her. Nobody knew what ailed her but me. In this struggle her health was quickly broken; her white face, attenuated form, and failing strength threatened rapid decline. I felt in my heart she would die if she did not go home, and with this conviction obtained her recall. She had only been three months at the school; and it was some years before the experiment of sending her from home was again ventured on.

Anne was sent for instead, but even with her younger sister at the school, Charlotte was desperately unhappy in her new job. Mary Taylor visited her there:

I HEARD THAT SHE HAD GONE as a teacher to Miss Wooler's. I went to see her, and asked how she could give so much for so little money, when she could live without it. She owned that after clothing herself and Anne, there was nothing left, though she had hoped to be able to save something. She confessed that it was not brilliant, but what could she do? I had nothing to answer. She seemed to have no interest or pleasure beyond the feeling of duty, and when she could get the opportunity, used to sit alone and 'make out' …

Writing was a compulsion and a necessity for Charlotte. It was to be so all her life, from the stories of Angria to her mature novels. She wrote in her journal:

OPPOSITE, ABOVE *One of the few representations of Anne Brontë, this delicate pencil drawing was sketched by Charlotte on 17 April 1833 when Anne was thirteen.*

OPPOSITE, BELOW *The diary paper which Emily and Anne Brontë wrote on 26 June 1837. The paper bears the mark of the creases where it would have been folded and put into the tin box which can be seen on the table where Emily and Anne are drawn writing, surrounded by diary papers. The papers were written about every four years, when the box would be opened and the old papers examined and read. All the papers weave daily happenings with the life of Gondal and predictions about what situation the family would be in when the next paper was written. In this case the forecast is optimistic: 'I guess that this day 4 years we shall all be in this drawing room comfortable – I hope it may be so – Anne guesses we shall all be gone somewhere together comfortable – We hope it may be so indeed.'*

I AM GOING TO WRITE because I cannot help it … encompassed by bulls (query calves of Bashan) all wondering why I write with my eyes shut – staring, gaping long in their astonishment. A C[ook] on one side of me, E L[ister] on the other and Miss W[ooler] in the background, stupidity the atmosphere, school-books the employment, assess the society. What in all this is there now to remind me of the divine, silent, unseen land of thought, dim now and indefinite as the dream of a dream, the shadow of a shade.

The incompatibility of the social and economic expectations of Charlotte's situation and her own private needs and abilities are nowhere better expressed than in her ironic response to Southey's advice that 'literature cannot be the business of a woman's life.' For Charlotte – and Emily and Anne, too – it was at its centre:

I THOUGHT IT … my duty, when I left school, to become a governess. In that capacity I find enough to occupy my thoughts all day long, and my head and hands too, without having a moment's time for one dream of the imagination. In the evenings, I confess, I do think, but I never trouble any one else with my thoughts. I carefully avoid any appearance of preoccupation and eccentricity, which might lead those I live amongst to suspect the nature of my pursuits … I have endeavoured not only attentively to observe all the duties a woman ought to fulfil, but to feel deeply interested in them. I don't always succeed, for sometimes I would rather be reading or writing; but I try to deny myself … I trust I shall never more feel ambitious to see my name in print; if the wish should rise, I'll look at Southey's letter and suppress it.

By February 1838, Charlotte's sense of isolation and alienation had brought her to the edge of a breakdown. She wrote to Ellen Nussey:

I OUGHT TO BE at Dewsbury Moor [the new location of Roe Head] you know, but I stayed as long as I was able, and at length I neither could nor dared stay any longer. My health and spirits utterly failed me, and the medical man whom I consulted enjoined me, if I valued my life, to go home. So home I went; the change has at once roused and soothed me, and I am now, I trust, fairly in the way to be myself again. A calm and even mind like yours, Ellen, cannot conceive the feelings of the shattered wretch who is writing to you …

The next few years were to see the Brontës making more and more hopeless rushes at the world of work, venturing from a home where they clung to each other and to their safe and discreet haven of spiritual peace and liberty into a world they were all singularly ill-equipped to deal with and where they sickened and failed. In Charlotte's words, '[I] became no better company than a stalking ghost … I felt my incapacity to *impart* pleasure fully as much as my powerlessness to receive it', and returned home again to recover and contemplate their next foray with dread.

While Charlotte was still at Roe Head, Emily had set out once again from the Parsonage, this time to go as a teacher at Law Hill School, a gaunt, dark house standing high up on the range of hills to the east of Halifax, some eight miles from Haworth. Charlotte wrote to Ellen:

EMILY IS GONE INTO A SITUATION as a teacher in a large school of nearly forty pupils near Halifax. I have had one letter from her since her departure; it gives an appalling account of her duties – hard labour from six in the morning until near eleven at night, with only one half hour of exercise between. This is slavery. I fear she will never stand it.

Emily managed to 'stand it' at Miss Patchett's school for about six months, hating teaching and succumbing to the sense of isolation and longing for Haworth that always engulfed her when she was away, which is reflected in the poem she wrote in the deserted classroom after her pupils were in bed:

ABOVE *View of Halifax from Beacon Hill. Law Hill, the Misses Patchett's school where Emily taught for some six months between September 1837 and March 1838, was situated in the nearby village of Southowram. The industrial town of Halifax lay nearly 1,000 feet down in the valley, wreathed in heavy black smoke, but the sunsets were glorious and Emily enjoyed horse riding during her time there.*

A LITTLE WHILE, a little while
The noisy crowd are barred away;
And I can sing and I can smile
A little while I've a holyday!

Where wilt thou go, my harassed heart?
Full many a land invites thee now;
And places near and far apart
Have rest for thee my weary brow.

There is a spot 'mid barren hills
Where winter howls and driving rain,
But if the dreary tempest chills
There is a light that warms again.

The house is old, the trees are bare
And moonless bends the misty dome
But what on earth is half as dear,
So longed for as the hearth of home?

By March 1839, Emily was back home at the Parsonage. Now it was Anne's turn. She was nineteen. Charlotte wrote to Ellen about her youngest sister's venture:

I COULD NOT WELL WRITE TO YOU in the week you requested as about that time we were very busy in preparing for Anne's departure – poor child! She left us last Monday. No one went with her – it was her own wish that she might be allowed to go alone – as she thought she could manage better and summon more courage if thrown entirely upon her own resources. We have had one letter from her since she went – she expresses herself very well satisfied, and says that Mrs Ingham is extremely kind; the two eldest children alone are under her care, the rest are confined to the nursery – with which and its occupants she has nothing to do. Both

RIGHT *'The governess received by a
Christian mother: She opened her
mouth with wisdom and in her tongue
is the law of kindness', an idealized
representation of the Victorian
governess's lot, replete with well-
behaved, eager-to-please children.
Neither Charlotte, Emily nor Anne
was ever able fully to come to terms
with the isolation and privations of
their various positions living in other
people's houses teaching other people's
ill-disposed children usually without
the necessary authority or support
from the parents. Anne reflected her
experiences in Agnes Grey: 'The
task of instruction was as arduous
for the body as the mind. I had to run
after my pupils to catch them, to carry
or drag them to the table, and often
forcibly hold them there till the lesson
was done.'*

her pupils are desperate little dunces – neither of them can read and sometimes they even profess a profound ignorance of their alphabet, the worst of it is the little monkies are excessively indulged and she is not empowered to inflict any punishment – she is requested when they misbehave themselves to inform their Mamma – which she says is utterly out of the question as in that case she might be making complaints from morning till night – 'So she alternately scolds, coaxes and threatens – sticks always to her first word and gets on as well as she can' – I hope she'll do, you would be astonished to see what a sensible, clever letter she writes …

Of all the Brontës, Anne seems to have been best able to survive life away from Haworth; her temperament was more stoical and she had a genuine fondness for children. But Anne had much to bear too. 'I have had some very unpleasant and un-dreamt of experiences of human nature,' she wrote in 1845, and the experiences she had as a governess were to form the substance of her novels.

Branwell, having taken further painting lessons in Leeds after his débâcle in London, was now trying his luck as a portrait painter in Bradford, lodging in the house of Mr Isaac Kirby, 'Porter & Ale Merchant' and his family, and coming home for weekends. The family were hopeful about this new venture, as Emily and Anne's diary paper from the previous June shows:

A BIT PAST 4 O'CLOCK, Charlotte working in Aunt's room, Branwell reading *Eugene Aram* to her – Anne and I writing in the drawing-room – All tight and right in which condition it is to be hoped we shall all be on this day 4 years at which time Charlotte will be 25 and 2 months – Branwell just 24 it being his birthday – myself 22 and 10 months and a piece Anne 21 and nearly a half I wonder where we shall be and what kind of a day it will be then let us hope for the best –

Charlotte, as the oldest, recognized her responsibility and in May 1839 she found a temporary position as a governess to the children of Mr and Mrs Sidgwick at Stonegappe near Skipton. Her letter to Emily (whom she here addresses as

ABOVE *Mrs Isaac Kirby, painted by Branwell. Branwell lodged with the Kirby family at 3, Fountain Street, Bradford, when he tried to establish himself as a portrait painter in 1838. The Kirbys were amongst his first commissions. A dispute developed over this portrait – probably painted in lieu of rent – which the Kirbys claimed Branwell had failed to varnish.*

Lavinia), shows that Charlotte would never be reconciled to the requirements and restraints of the task of the governess:

I HAVE STRIVEN HARD to be pleased with my new situation. The country, the house, and the grounds are, as I have said, divine. But, alack-a-day! there is such a thing as seeing all beautiful around you – pleasant woods, winding white paths, green lawns, and blue sunshiny sky – and not having a free moment or a free thought left to enjoy them … I said in my last letter that Mrs Sidgwick did not know me. I now begin to find that she does not intend to know me, that she cares nothing in the world about me except to contrive how the greatest possible quantity of labour may be squeezed out of me, and to that end she overwhelms me with oceans of needlework, yards of cambric to hem, muslin nightcaps to make, and, above all things, dolls to dress. I do not think she likes me at all, because I can't help being shy in such an entirely novel scene, surrounded as I have hitherto been by strange and constantly changing faces. I used to think I should like to be in the stir of grand folks' society but I have had enough of it – it is dreary work to look on and listen. I see now more clearly than I have ever done before that a private governess has no existence, is not considered as a living and rational being except as connected with the wearisome duties she has to fulfil. While she is teaching the children, working for them, amusing them, it is all right. If she steals a moment for herself she is a nuisance.

Charlotte wrote to Emily again in July:

MINE BONNIE LOVE, I was as glad of your letter as tongue can express: it is a real, genuine pleasure to hear from home; a thing to be saved until bedtime, when one has a moment's quiet and rest to enjoy it thoroughly. Write whenever you can. I could like to be at home. I could like to work in a mill. I could like to feel mental liberty. I could like this weight of restraint to be taken off. But the holidays will come. Coraggio.

RIGHT *'How beautiful is the smoke/ The Bradford smoke:/Pouring from numberless chimney-stacks, / Condensing and falling in showers of "blacks",/All around/Upon the ground,' a satirist wrote of Bradford, one of the great woollen towns of Victorian England. It had a reputation for radicalism and, like Manchester, a 'propensity to riot'. 'We don't live in the days of Barons, thank God,' exclaimed the Whig Lord Brougham in 1830. 'We live in the days of Leeds, of Bradford, of Halifax and of Huddersfield.' This monument to progress – with its dark underside of poverty – was the nearest city to Haworth, and was a staging post for the Brontës on the small circles they inscribed around the Pennines when making occasional visits to family and friends.*

By the end of July Charlotte was home again. She had been away for only two months. But if Stonegappe had proved another humiliating experience for Charlotte as a teacher, it was to prove useful to Charlotte as a writer: the odious John Reed in *Jane Eyre* was probably suggested by the behaviour of Benson Sidgwick; while a nearby house, Norton Conyers, with its own 'mad woman' legend, which Charlotte visited at the time, is occasionally identified with Mr Rochester's residence, Thornfield Hall.

For the next eighteen months, Charlotte stayed at the Parsonage, with Emily, sometimes Branwell, and Anne, who had now returned from her job with the Ingham family at Blake Hall, Mirfield. There was plenty to keep the returners occupied, as Charlotte wrote to Ellen Nussey on 21 December 1839:

> WE ARE AT PRESENT and have been during the last month rather busy as for that space of time we have been without a servant except for a girl to run errands – poor Tabby – she became so lame from a large ulcer in her leg that she was at length obliged to leave us – is residing with her Sister in a little house of her own … In the meantime Emily and I are sufficiently busy as you may suppose – I manage the ironing and keep the rooms clean – Emily does the baking and attends to the Kitchen – We are such odd animals that we prefer this mode of contrivance to having a new face among us. Besides we do not despair of Tabby's return and she shall not be supplanted by a stranger in her absence. I excited Aunt's wrath very much by burning the cloth[e]s the first time I attempted to Iron but I do better now. Human beings are queer things – I am much happier – black-leading the stoves, making the beds and sweeping the floors at home – than I should be living like a fine lady anywhere else.

But Charlotte recognized that they must 'try again', and on 2 March 1841 she went as governess to children of the White family at Upperwood House, Rawdon, Leeds, whilst Anne travelled further afield at the end of the same month, seventy miles to Thorp Green Hall, Little Ouseburn, just outside York, where she took up a position with the Robinson family.

ABOVE *In 1895 the Reverend Arthur Nicholls wrote to a biographer of the Brontës referring to the diary papers he had found: 'The four small scraps of Emily and Anne's MSS I found in the small box I send you. They are sad reading, poor girls!' These illustrations are from the diary dated 30 July 1841.*

OPPOSITE *Anne made this contribution to the diary paper from Scarborough, where she was on a visit from Thorp Green: 'What will the next four years bring forth? Providence only knows. But we ourselves have sustained very little alteration ... I have the same faults ... only I have more wisdom and experience, and a little more self-possession than I then enjoyed ...'*

RIGHT *Little Ouseburn Church, a pencil sketch by Anne Brontë of the village church nearest to Thorp Green Hall, which Anne attended whilst she was a governess to the children of the Robinson family: Mary, Lydia, Elizabeth, Edmund – and a baby, Georgiana. Anne stayed for five years, despite confiding in her diary in 1841, 'I dislike this situation and wish to change it.'*

But the prospect of a lifetime spent governessing in other people's houses for scant respect, low wages, far from home and with a deadening curtailment of 'mental liberty' was bleak. And in that year, 1841, Charlotte, Emily and Anne began to discuss an alternative.

CHAPTER 4
THE WORLD WITHOUT

'THERE IS A PROJECT hatching in this house,' Charlotte wrote to Ellen on 19 July 1841, 'which both Emily and I anxiously wished to discuss with you. The project is yet in its infancy, hardly peeping from its shell; and whether it will ever come out a fine full-fledged chicken, or will turn addle, and die before it cheeps, is one of those considerations that are but dimly revealed by the oracles of futurity … To come to the point, papa and aunt talk, by fits and starts, of our – *id est*, Emily, Anne, and myself – commencing a school. I have often, you know, said how much I wished such a thing; but I never could conceive where the capital was to come from for making such a speculation. I was well aware, indeed, that aunt had money, but I always considered that she was the last person who would offer a loan for the purpose in question. A loan, however, she *has* offered, or rather intimates that she perhaps *will* offer, in case pupils can be secured, an eligible situation obtained, etc.'

At first a suggestion to Charlotte from the former headmistress of Roe Head seemed feasible:

> MISS WOOLER DID MOST KINDLY PROPOSE that I should come to Dewsbury Moor and attempt to revive the school her sister had relinquished – she offered me the use of her furniture for the consideration of her board – at first I received the proposal cordially and proposed to do my utmost to bring about success – but a fire was kindled in my very heart which I could not quench – I so longed to increase my attainments to become something better than I am – a glimpse of what I felt shewed to you in one of my former letters – only a glimpse – Mary Taylor cast oil on the flames – encouraged me and in her own strong energetic language heartened me on – I longed to go to Brussels – but how could l get? I wished for one at least of my Sisters to share the advantage with me, I fixed on Emily …

OPPOSITE A Packet Boat *by James Taylor.* La Malle Anglaise, *as the Ostend packet was called, sailed from London Bridge Wharf on Wednesdays and Saturdays, often weighing anchor before dawn to catch the tide. Charlotte and Emily Brontë came down to London on Tuesday 8 February 1842 ready to make the fourteen-hour long sea crossing to Belgium the following Saturday. In* Villette *Lucy Snowe recounts that she was 'not sick till long after we passed Margate, and deep was the pleasure I drank in with the sea-breeze; divine the delight I drew from the heaving channel-waves, from the sea-birds on their ridges, from the white sails on their dark distance, from the quiet, yet beclouded sky, overhanging all.'*

OPPOSITE *As their stagecoach drew near to Brussels, some forty miles from Ostend, one of the first sights that Charlotte and Emily would have seen was the 364-foot tower, surmounted with a copper figure of St Michael, seventeen feet high, which turned in the wind, atop the medieval Hôtel de Ville in the city's Grande Place. 'Brussels is a beautiful city,' Charlotte confirmed in a letter to Ellen Nussey.*

Charlotte explained her change of mind in a most business-like letter to her Aunt Branwell:

MY FRIENDS RECOMMEND ME, if I desire to secure permanent success, to delay commencing the school for six months longer, and by all means to contrive, by hook or by crook, to spend the intervening time in some school on the Continent. They say schools in England are so numerous, competition so great, that without some such step towards attaining superiority we shall probably have a very hard struggle, and may fail in the end. They say, moreover, that the loan of £100, which you have been so kind as to offer us, will, perhaps, not be all required now, as Miss Wooler will lend us the furniture; and that, if the speculation is intended to be a good and successful one, half the sum, at least, ought to be laid out in the manner I have mentioned, thereby insuring a more speedy repayment both of interest and principal.

I would not go to France or to Paris. I would go to Brussels, in Belgium. The cost of the journey there, at the dearest rate of travelling, would be £5; living is there little more than half as dear as it is in England, and the facilities for education are equal or superior to any other place in Europe. In half a year, I could acquire a thorough familiarity with French. I could improve greatly in Italian, and even get a dash of German, i.e. providing my health continued as good as it is now. Martha Taylor is now staying in Brussels, at a first-rate establishment there. I should not think of going to the Chateau de Kockleberg, where she is resident, as the terms are much too high …

These are advantages which would turn to vast account, when we actually commenced a school – and, if Emily could share them with me, only for a single half-year, we could take a footing in the world afterwards which we can never do now … I know no other friend in the world to whom I could apply on this subject except yourself. I feel an absolute conviction that, if this advantage were allowed us, it would be the making of us for life. Papa will perhaps think it a wild and ambitious scheme; but who ever rose in the world without ambition? When he left Ireland to go to Cambridge University, he was as ambitious as I am now. I want us *all* to go on. I know we have talents, and I want them to be turned to account. I look to you, aunt, to help us. I think you will not refuse. I know, if you consent, it shall not be my fault if you ever repent your kindness.

Although 'people everywhere are hard to spur up the proper speed', the Brussels plan was a reality by Christmas. Charlotte relinquished her job with the Whites, and on 8 February 1842 she and Emily, accompanied by their father and Mary Taylor and her brother, Joe, left Haworth to take the packet to Ostend and on to Brussels. They were bound for the rue d'Isabelle where 'in the thirteenth century … the ducal kennels occupied the place where Madame Heger's pensionnat now stands.' This is where they stayed, and Charlotte described their life at the Pensionnat Heger in a letter to Ellen:

I WAS TWENTY-SIX YEARS OLD, a week or two since, and at this ripe time of life I am a schoolgirl, a complete schoolgirl, and, on the whole, very happy in that capacity. It felt very strange at first to submit to authority instead of exercising it – to obey orders instead of giving them; but I like that state of things. I returned to it with the same avidity that a cow, that has long

OPPOSITE Whilst the pupils and teachers of the Pensionnat Heger left for the country in the summer vacation, Charlotte Brontë stayed on in the empty school, alone in a foreign country. She wrote to Emily on 2 September 1843: 'I have ramped around a great deal and tried to get a clearer acquaintance with the streets of Bruxelles … I should inevitably fall into a gulf of low spirits if I stayed always by myself here without a human being to speak to, so I go out and traverse the Boulevards and streets of Bruxelles sometimes for hours together', passing, no doubt, la Fontaine de Manneken Pis (shown here), a popular tourist attraction.

LEFT 'You ask about Queen Victoria's visit to Brussels,' wrote Charlotte to Emily after her return to Belgium in 1843. 'I saw her for an instant flashing through the Rue Royale [shown here] in a carriage and six, surrounded by soldiers. She was laughing and talking very gaily. She looked a little stout, vivacious lady, very plainly dressed, not much dignity or pretension about her. The Belgians liked her very well on the whole. They said she enlivened the sombre court of King Leopold, which is usually as gloomy as a conventicle.'

FONTAINE DU MANNEKEN-PIS, A BRUXELLES

LEFT *An illustration for* Villette *by E. M. Wimperis. On her arrival in the city, Lucy Snowe, almost penniless, searched for an inn: 'In a very quiet and comparatively clean and well-paved street, I saw a light burning over the door of a rather large house … This might be the inn at last. I hastened on: my knees now trembled under me: I was getting quite exhausted. No inn was this. A brass-plate embellished the great Porte-cochère: 'Pensionnat de Demoiselles' was the inscription; and beneath, a name, 'Madame Beck' … I rung the door-bell.' Charlotte based the 'Pensionnat de Demoiselles' on the Pensionnat Heger in the Rue d'Isabelle in Brussels, where she and Emily had been pupils.*

been kept on dry hay, returns to fresh grass. Don't laugh at my simile. It is natural to me to submit, and very unnatural to command.

This is a large school, in which there are about forty *externes* or day-pupils, and twelve *pensionnaires* or boarders. Madame Heger, the head, is a lady of precisely the same cast of mind, degree of cultivation, and quality of intellect as Miss Catherine Wooler. I think the severe points are a little softened, because she has not been disappointed, and consequently soured. In a word, she is a married instead of a maiden lady. There are three teachers in the school – Mademoiselle Blanche, Mademoiselle Sophie, and Mademoiselle Marie. The two first have no particular character. One is an old maid, and the other will be one. Mademoiselle Marie is talented and original, but of repulsive and arbitrary manners, which have made the whole school, except myself and Emily, her bitter enemies. No less than seven masters attend to teach the different branches of education – French, Drawing, Music, Singing, Writing, Arithmetic, and German. All in the house are Catholics except ourselves, one other girl, and the *gouvernante* of Madame's children, an English woman, in rank something between a lady's-maid and nursery governess. The difference in country and religion makes a broad line of demarcation between us and all the rest. We are completely isolated in the midst of numbers. Yet I think I am never unhappy; my present life is so delightful, so congenial to my own nature, compared with that of a governess. My time, constantly occupied, passes too rapidly. Hitherto both Emily and I have had good health, and therefore we have been able to work well.

Some years later, Mrs Gaskell heard M. Heger's rather different account of Charlotte and Emily at this time:

THE TWO SISTERS clung together, and kept apart from the herd of happy, boisterous, well-befriended Belgian girls, who, in their turn, thought the new English pupils wild and scared-looking, with strange, odd, insular ideas about dress; for Emily had taken a fancy to the fashion, ugly and preposterous even during its reign, of gigot sleeves and persisted in wearing them long after they were 'gone out'. Her petticoats, too, had not a curve or a wave in them, but hung down straight and long, clinging to her lank figure. The sisters spoke to no one but from necessity. They were too full of earnest thought, and of the exile's sick yearning, to be ready for careless conversation, or merry game. M. Heger ... perceived that with their unusual characters, and extraordinary talents, a different mode must be adopted from that in which he generally taught French to English girls [Charlotte and Emily at twenty-six and twenty-four were considerably older than the other pupils, a fact that was acknowledged in their sleeping arrangements, for the sisters slept curtained off at the end of the long dormitory]. He seems to have rated Emily's genius as something

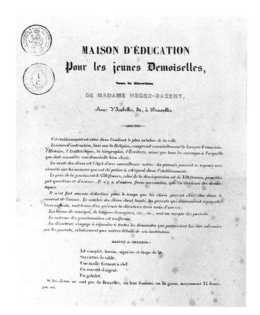

ABOVE *The prospectus of the Pensionnat Heger, which stressed the salubrious district of Brussels in which the school was situated and the accomplishments its curriculum would instil in the young ladies who enrolled as pupils. Madame Beck in* Villette *is modelled on Madame Zoë Heger, who owned the school.*

even higher than Charlotte's … Emily had a head for logic, and a capability for argument, unusual in a man, and rare indeed in a woman, according to M. Heger. Impairing the force of this gift was a stubborn tenacity of will, which rendered her obtuse to all reasoning where her own wishes, or her own sense of right, was concerned. 'She should have been a man – a great navigator,' said M. Heger in speaking of her. 'Her powerful reason would have deduced new spheres of discovery from the knowledge of the old; and her strong imperious will would never have been daunted by opposition or difficulty; never have given way but with life.'

Charlotte recognized the ordeal it was for Emily to be so far from her beloved Haworth and subject again to society:

> ONCE MORE SHE SEEMED SINKING, but this time she rallied through mere force of resolution: with inward remorse and shame she looked back on her former failure, and resolved to conquer in this second ordeal. She did conquer: but the victory cost her dear. She was never happy till she carried her hard-won knowledge back to the remote English village, the old parsonage-house, and desolate Yorkshire hills.

Charlotte and Emily were indeed 'completely isolated in the midst of numbers' – even when they went out visiting the British chaplain and his wife, the visits caused the girls 'more pain than pleasure … Emily hardly uttered more than a monosyllable', whilst Charlotte 'had a habit of gradually wheeling round in her chair, so as almost to conceal her face from the person to whom she was speaking' – yet they were

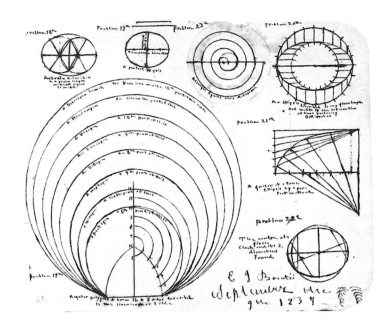

ABOVE *A page of geometrical drawings by Emily Brontë, dated 9 September 1837. It was Emily, who M. Heger thought 'should have been a man – a great navigator', so logical was her mind, who was entrusted to look after the Brontë sisters' investment in railway shares, the venture into which they had sunk their Aunt Branwell's legacy. Charlotte wrote to Miss Wooler in 1845: 'Emily has made herself mistress of the necessary degree of knowledge for conducting the matter, by dint of careful reading of every paragraph and every advertisement in the news papers that related to rail-roads, and as we have abstained from all gambling, all mere speculative buying-in and selling-out – we have got on very decently.'*

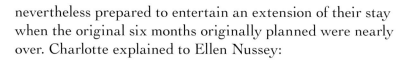

RIGHT *In later years, M. Heger recalled Charlotte and Emily Brontë as being 'wild and scared-looking with odd insular ideas about dress', especially a liking for 'ugly and preposterous', and by then unfashionable, gigot sleeves (as in this fashion plate). It seems unlikely, however, that a woman who wrote, 'Riches I hold in light esteem/And Love I laugh to scorn/And lust of fame was but a dream/That vanished with the morn', would be overly concerned with the sartorial approbation of others.*

nevertheless prepared to entertain an extension of their stay when the original six months originally planned were nearly over. Charlotte explained to Ellen Nussey:

I CONSIDER IT DOUBTFUL whether I shall come home in September or not – Madame Heger has made a proposal for both me and Emily to stay another half year – offering to dismiss her English master and take me as English teacher – also to employ Emily some part of each day as in teaching music to a certain number of the pupils – for these services we are to be allowed to continue our studies in French and German – and have board without paying for it – no salaries however are offered – the proposal is kind and in a great selfish city like Brussels and a great selfish school containing nearly ninety pupils (boarders and day-pupils included) implies a degree of interest which demands gratitude in return – I am inclined to accept it – what think you?

But events at home dictated otherwise. On 10 November 1842, nine months after they had arrived in Brussels, Charlotte wrote to Ellen:

WE RECEIVED THE FIRST NEWS of aunt's illness, Wednesday, Nov. 2nd. We decided to come home directly. Next morning a second letter informed us of her death. We sailed from Antwerp on Sunday; we travelled day and night and got home on Tuesday morning – and of course the funeral and all was over. We shall see her no more.

Miss Branwell's was the third death that autumn that was to graze the lives of the Brontës, In September, Charlotte and Emily had received news that the Reverend William Weightman had died of cholera aged twenty-eight. Cholera epidemics were an all too frequent occurrence at Haworth, where the poor sanitation meant that the virus washed down the hill from the graveyard in a closed circuit of sickness and death. Mr Weightman had been a curate at Haworth since 1839. He was a 'bright lad', jovial, flirtatious and somewhat effeminate, with a pink and white complexion and auburn curls. Charlotte christened him Miss Celia Amelia and was sardonic about his amatory tendencies: 'a thorough going male flirt … [who] will never want for troops of victims amongst young ladies', but he was a good friend to Branwell, who wept bitterly at his funeral. It is possible that Anne had fallen in love with Mr Weightman, and he with her. As Charlotte recorded in a letter to Ellen:

> HE SITS OPPOSITE ANNE at church sighing softly and looking out of the
> corners of his eyes to win her attentions – and Anne is so quiet,
> her look so downcast – they are a picture.

Soon after his death, Anne, who was away at Thorp Green when the curate had finally 'run [his] bright but short career', wrote:

> I WILL NOT MOURN thee, lovely one,
> Though thou art torn away.
> 'Tis said that if the morning sun
> Arise with dazzling ray …
>
> And if thy life as transient proved,
> It hath been full as bright,
> For thou wert hopeful and beloved;
> Thy spirit knew no blight.

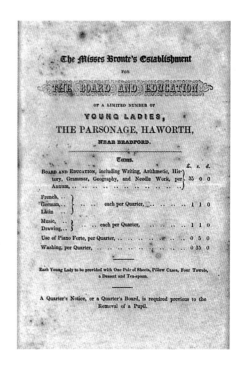

ABOVE *In 1844 Charlotte had a prospectus printed for the Brontës' proposed school. She canvassed reactions: 'Mrs Busfeild thought the undertaking a most praiseworthy one, but feared I should have some difficulty in making it succeed on account of the situation. Such is the answer I receive from almost everyone.'*

With his gossip, attention and valentines, Miss Celia Amelia had brought life and youthful gaiety to the Parsonage which had seen little before, and would see less in the next few years.

Another spark went out of Charlotte and Emily's lives when 'little Miss Boisterous', Martha Taylor, died suddenly in October at the pension at Koekelberg where she and Mary were studying. She was buried at the Protestant cemetery, outside Brussels, a place which had a powerful effect on Charlotte who described it in *The Professor*, and suffused her description of the funeral of Jessy York in *Shirley* with her feelings of strangeness at the Dissenter's grave in Belgium:

> A HOWLING, RAINY AUTUMN EVENING … when certain who had that day performed a pilgrimage to a grave new-made in a heretic cemetery, sat near a woodfire on the hearth of a foreign dwelling … they knew that heavy falling rain was soaking into the wet earth which covered their lost darling: and that the sad, sighing gale was mourning above her buried head …

Aunt Branwell's will was proved in December 1842. The sisters each received a legacy of about £300 – a sum insufficient to make them independent, but enough for them to press ahead with their school project in earnest.

The sad homecoming was made sadder when Emily discovered that in her absence her aunt had disposed of part of her menagerie:

ABOVE *Martha Taylor, Mary's younger sister, died of cholera in Brussels in October 1842. The Taylors were Dissenters so Martha was buried in the Protestant cemetery on the outskirts of the city. Charlotte was much affected when she visited the cemetery, both by the consciousness of her own losses ('Aunt, Martha Taylor, and Mr Weightman are now all gone; how dreary and void everything seems') and by a sense of alienation: 'I have seen Martha's grave – the place where her ashes lie in a foreign country' – and a popish Catholic one too in Charlotte's view. She fictionalized these feelings powerfully in* Shirley *and also in* The Professor *(illustrated here).*

WE HAVE GOT FLOSSY; got and lost Tiger; lost the hawk Hero, which, with the geese, was given away, and is doubtless dead, for when I came back from Brussels I inquired on all hands and could hear nothing of him … Keeper and Flossy are well, also the canary acquired four years since.

Yet, she was profoundly relieved to be back at Haworth. She took charge of the household and:

TOOK THE PRINCIPAL PART of the cooking on herself, and did all the household ironing; and after Tabby grew old and infirm, it was Emily who made all the bread for the family and anyone passing by the kitchen door might have seen her studying German out of an open book, propped up before her as she kneaded the dough; but no study, however interesting, interfered with the goodness of the bread, which was always light and excellent.

Emily was never to leave the Parsonage again. Self-sufficient and silent, she had a need for solitude and the wild moors that was overwhelming. Flourishing in the world she created in her own mind, she wrote a poem 'To Imagination' in September 1844 when she was alone with her father at Haworth:

SO HOPELESS is the world without,
The world within I doubly prize;
Thy world where guile and hate and doubt
And cold suspicion never rise;
Where thou and I and liberty
Have undisputed sovereignty.

ABOVE *A watercolour study by Emily Brontë of her bull mastiff. 'The tawny, strong-limbed Keeper [was] Emily's favourite; he was completely under her control, she could quite easily make him spring or roar like a lion.' Almost Emily's last act, four days before she died, was to feed Keeper, and the dog 'walked alongside of the mourners' to her funeral.*

OPPOSITE *An undated watercolour by Charlotte Brontë depicting a black and white spaniel chasing a bird across moorland. It is thought to be a portrayal of Flossy, the dog given to Anne by the Robinson children to whom she had been governess at Thorp Green. The spaniel outlived Anne by many years, dying in 1854.*

But Charlotte was resolved to return to Brussels. It was a courageous decision for someone as shy as she was to set off for Belgium again alone. As she was rowed out to the Ostend packet riding at anchor, the sea at night and the enormity of her enterprise made her think of:

> THE STYX, OR CHARION ROWING some solitary soul to the Land of the Shades. Amidst the strange scene, with a chilly wind blowing in my face and midnight-clouds dropping rain above my head; with two rude rowers for companions, whose insane oaths still tortured my ears, I asked myself if I was wretched or terrified. I was neither … I could not tell how I was.

Charlotte had written to Ellen Nussey on 6 March 1842:

> I AM SETTLED by this time, of course. I am not too much overloaded with occupation; and besides teaching English I have time to improve myself in German. I ought to consider myself well off, and to be thankful for my good fortune.

A subsequent letter shows her less equanimous:

> THERE ARE PRIVATIONS and humiliations to submit to – there is monotony and uniformity of life – and above all there is a constant sense of solitude in the midst of numbers – the Protestant and the Foreigner is a solitary being whether as teacher or pupil.

Charlotte gradually became more and more unhappy, as she explained in a letter to Branwell:

OPPOSITE *Charlotte Brontë always thought of herself as plain. In an Angrian story she describes her* alter ego, *Charlotte Wiggins, as 'a broad dumpy thing whose head does not come higher than my [Branwell's] elbow', and when she wrote* Jane Eyre *she made the heroine 'as small and plain as myself.' At the end of a letter Charlotte wrote to Ellen Nussey from Brussels on 6 March 1843, she sketched this stunted, ugly figure, labelling it 'C. Brontë', waving goodbye to Ellen Nussey; portrayed as a quintessential beauty with a tall, bespectacled admirer, identified as 'The Chosen', clearly a current suitor of Ellen's.*

I CAN DISCERN only one or two [pupils and fellow teachers] who deserve anything like regard … They have not intellect or politeness or good-nature or good-feeling. They are nothing … They have no sensation themselves and they excite none. But one wearies from day to day of caring nothing, fearing nothing, liking nothing, hating nothing, being nothing, doing nothing – yes, I teach and sometimes get red in the face with impatience at their stupidity. But I don't think that I ever scold or fly into a passion. If I spoke warmly, as warmly as I sometimes used to do at Roe Head, they would think me mad. Nobody ever gets into a passion here. Such a thing is not known. The phlegm that thickens their blood is too gluey to boil.

It was, however, not just the stupidity of her pupils and colleagues, nor the leadenness of the Belgian people, nor even the turmoil in that she despised and yet was strangely drawn towards the Catholic Church, that made Charlotte write:

BRUSSELS, SATURDAY MORNING, Oct. 14th 1843. First Class. I am very cold – there is no Fire – I wish I were at home with Papa – Branwell – Emily – Anne & Tabby – I am tired of being among foreigners. It is a dreary life – especially as there is only one person in this house worthy of being liked – also another, who seems a rosy sugar plum but I know her to be coloured chalk.

The 'sugar plum' was Mme Heger – whom Charlotte would later metamorphose as Zoraide Reuter in *The Professor* and Mme Beck in *Villette*. She treated Charlotte with a cold formality, and retracted her earlier friendly overtures when she perceived that Charlotte had fallen in love with 'the only person in this house worthy of being liked', her husband, Constantin Heger, whom Charlotte called the 'black swan' and on whom she modelled Paul Emmanuel in *Villette*. On her first acquaintance with the teacher, Charlotte's impression had been of:

A PROFESSOR OF RHETORIC, a man of power as to mind, but very choleric and irritable as to temperament; a little black, ugly being, with a face that varies in expression. Sometimes he is a delirious hyena; occasionally, but very seldom, he discards these perilous attractions and assumes an air not above 100 degrees removed from mild and gentleman-like.

But she was soon to find his intellect stimulating and exhilarating, and his charm compelling, and she strove to please him as a pupil. After her return to Brussels as a teacher – though she still continued her German lessons, and at first gave English lessons to M. Heger – Charlotte found the changes in her relationship with her former teacher mortifying and confusing, all the more so because her strong attachment to him remained unacknowledged – perhaps even to herself:

> I RARELY SPEAK to Monsieur now, for not being a pupil I have little or nothing to do with him. From time to time he shows his kind-heartedness by loading me with books, so that I am still indebted to him for all the pleasure and amusement that I have.

But despite M. Heger's distant manner and Mme Heger's *froideur* and the entreaties of her family, Charlotte stayed on, unhappily, at the Pensionnat; it was to be nearly a whole lonely and painful year after she had arrived in Brussels for the second time until Charlotte wrote to Emily on 19 December 1843 that 'I have taken my determination. I hope to be at home the day after New Year's Day. I have told Mme Heger …' On her return to Haworth, Charlotte wrote frequently to M. Heger, and even though he soon instructed her that she must write to him only on matters of daily interest, not try to engage him with her feelings, and a letter was to be sent only twice a year, her deep and continuing infatuation for him was expressed for the first time in these painful letters:

> THE SIX MONTHS OF silence have run their course. It is now the 18th of Novr.; my last letter was dated (I think) the 18th of May. I may therefore write to you again without failing in my promise.

ABOVE *The envelope from one of the letters Charlotte Brontë posted to M. Heger from Haworth between January 1844 and November 1845. Despite entreaties to her former teacher, a reply never arrived.*

RIGHT The Heger Family, *painted by Ange François in 1847, five years after Charlotte had first met them. Back row, left to right: Prosper, Louise; front row, left to right: Victorine, Madame Zoë Parent Heger, Paul, Marie and Claire; Constantin Heger stands apart from his family (back left). On her return to Brussels without Emily, Charlotte felt excluded from the Hegers' family life: 'M. and Madame Heger are the only two persons in the house for whom I really experience esteem, and, of course, I cannot always be with them, nor even often. They told me ... that I was to consider their sitting-room my sitting-room also, and go there whenever I was not engaged in the schoolroom. This, however, I cannot do. In the daytime it is a public room ... and in the evening I will not and ought not to intrude on M. and Madame Heger and their children.'*

The summer and autumn seemed very long to me; truth to tell, it has needed painful efforts on my part to bear hitherto the self-denial which I have imposed on myself. You, monsieur, you cannot conceive what it means …

I tell you frankly that I have tried meanwhile to forget you, for the remembrance of a person whom one thinks never to see again and whom, nevertheless, one greatly esteems, frets too much the mind; and when one has suffered that kind of anxiety for a year or two, one is ready to do anything to find peace once more. I have done everything; I have sought occupations; I have denied myself absolutely the pleasure of speaking about you – even to Emily; but I have been able to conquer neither my regrets nor my impatience. That indeed is humiliating – to be unable to control one's own thoughts, to be the slave of a regret, of a memory, the slave of a fixed and dominant idea which lords it over the mind …

Monsieur, I have a favour to ask of you; when you reply to this letter, speak to me a little of yourself, not of me; for I know that if you speak of me it will be to scold me, and this time I would see your kindly side. Speak to me therefore of your children … Tell me also something of the School, of the pupils, of the Governesses … Tell me where you travelled during the holidays – did

OPPOSITE *On 8 January 1845 Charlotte wrote a further letter to the silent, unresponsive M. Heger which demonstrated the fluency of her French and the anguish of her feelings: 'Day and night I find neither peace nor rest. If I sleep I am disturbed by tormenting dreams in which I see you, always severe, always grave, always incensed with me … If my master withdraws his friendship from me entirely I shall be altogether without hope; if he gives me a little – just a little – I shall be satisfied – happy; I shall have a reason for living on, for working.' M. Heger read the letter, tore it up and threw the pieces in the wastepaper basket. Mme Heger fished out and reassembled the pieces and painstakingly stitched them together again before stowing the letter carefully away.*

you go to the Rhine? Did you not visit Cologne or Coblentz? Tell me, in short, my master, what you will, but tell me something. To write to an ex-assistant-governess (No! I refuse to remember my employment as an assistant-governess – I repudiate it) – anyhow, to write to an old pupil cannot be a very interesting occupation for you, I know; but for me it is life. Your last letter was stay and prop to me – nourishment to me for half a year. Now I need another … to forbid me to write to you, to refuse to answer me, would be to tear from me my only joy on earth, to deprive me of my last privilege – a privilege I shall never consent willingly to surrender … When day by day I await a letter and when day by day disappointment comes to fling me back to overwhelming sorrow, and the sweet delight of seeing your handwriting and reading your counsel escapes me as a vision that is vain, then fever claims me – I lose appetite and sleep – I pine away.

May I write to you again next May? I would rather wait a year, but it is impossible – it is too long.

There was no word in reply, and in the margin of this letter from Charlotte, M. Heger scribbled the name and address of a shoemaker he had been recommended.

Anne was feeling uncertain and anxious about the future, too, as she wrote in her customary four-year diary paper:

THIS IS A DISMAL, cloudy, wet evening. We have had so far a very cold, wet summer. Charlotte has lately been to Hathersage, in Derbyshire, on a visit of three weeks to Ellen Nussey. She is now sitting sewing in the dining-room. Emily is ironing upstairs. I am sitting in the dining-room in the rocking-chair before the fire with my feet on the fender. Papa is in the parlour. Tabby and Martha are, I think, in the kitchen. Keeper and Flossy are, I do not know where. Little Dick is hopping in his cage. When the last paper was written we were thinking of setting up a school. The scheme has been dropt, and long after taken up again, and dropt again, because we could not get pupils. Charlotte is thinking about getting another situation. She wishes to go to Paris. Will she go? … I wonder how we shall all be, and where and how situated, on the thirtieth of July 1848, when, if we are all alive, Emily will be just 30. I shall be in my 29th year, Charlotte in her 33rd, and Branwell in his 32nd; and what changes shall we have seen and known; and shall we be much changed ourselves? I hope not, for the worse at least. I for my part cannot well be flatter or older in mind than I am now. Hoping for the best, I conclude.

By the end of the year, Charlotte, Emily, Branwell and Anne were all home at the Parsonage with their father. But this was not a time of contentment. Charlotte, bruised by her experiences in Brussels, accompanied her father to Manchester to consult an ophthalmic surgeon about his increasing short-sightedness, and to add to her feelings of isolation and despair, she recognized that she had lost her childhood partner in Angria, her brother, Branwell. The 'family genius', the bright hope of their ambition, had come to nothing.

His career as an artist had never progressed beyond a few portraiture commissions; despite the encouragement he received from Hartley Coleridge (the poet's son) when Branwell sent him his translations of the Odes of Horace, he was to receive no such enthusiasm when he wrote first to the editor of *Blackwood's Magazine* and then to the poet William Wordsworth, aggressively soliciting their help and advice to further his literary career. His employment as a clerk with the new railway company, first at Sowerby and then at

ABOVE *Whilst Branwell Brontë was employed as a clerk at Luddenden Foot station on the Leeds–Manchester railway, he was required to keep a notebook detailing the trains that passed through the station and the freight they carried. He was dismissed from this post in March 1842 when a discrepancy was discovered in the accounts. It is unlikely that Branwell himself had stolen the money, but his notebook is evidence of the charge of carelessness that was levelled against him.*

ABOVE *John Brown was the sexton at Haworth and a stonemason who carved headstones for the churchyard. A learned man, who could vie with 'Mr Brontë himself in his knowledge of dead languages', he was a good friend and drinking companion of Branwell, who painted this portrait.*

Luddenden Foot, came to an abrupt end in 1843 when Branwell was dismissed for 'irregularities' (gross neglect rather than actual dishonesty). The final humiliation came when he was summarily dismissed from the post Anne had secured for him as tutor to one of the Robinson children at Thorp Green near Kirby, where she was a governess for five years. Branwell gave his own account of the circumstances in a letter to the friend he had made at Luddenden Foot, Francis Grundy, in October 1845:

> I WAS TUTOR to the son of a wealthy gentleman [Mr Edmund Robinson, Thorp Green Hall] whose wife is sister to the wife of – – – , M.P., for the county of – – – … This lady (though her husband detested me) showed me a degree of kindness which, when I was deeply grieved one day at her husband's conduct, ripened into declarations of more than ordinary feeling. My admiration of her mental and personal attractions, my knowledge of her unselfish sincerity, her sweet temper, and unwearied care for others … although she is seventeen years my senior, all combined to an attachment on my part, and led to reciprocations which I had little looked for. During nearly three years I had daily 'troubled pleasure soon chastised by fear.' Three months since, I received a furious letter from my employer, threatening to shoot me if I returned from my vacation which I was passing at home … I have lain during nine long weeks utterly shattered in body and broken down in mind. The probability of her becoming free to give me herself and estate never rose to drive away the prospect of her decline under her present grief. I dreaded, too, the wreck of my mind and body, which God knows during a short life have been severely tried … You will say 'What a fool!' but if you knew the many causes I have for sorrow which I cannot even hint at here, you would perhaps pity as well as blame.

Branwell's undoubted talents had for some time been displayed only to his drinking companions. One such was John Brown, his father's sexton, and a

member of the same masonic lodge as Branwell, whom he addressed as 'Old Knave of Trumps' when he wrote of his exploits:

> THERE WAS A PARTY of gentlemen at the Royal Hotel, and I joined them. We ordered supper and whisky-toddy as 'hot as hell!'. They thought I was a physician, and put me in the chair. I gave sundry toasts, that were washed down at the same time, till the room spun round and the candles danced in our eyes.

Another was the landlord of the Black Bull in Haworth, who would send for the Parson's son to entertain new customers with his excitable eloquence and his ambidextrous ability, allegedly writing Latin with his left hand, whilst simultaneously penning Greek with his right. But at home his sisters saw the

ABOVE *Two pugilists stripped bare to the waist, a sketch dated 3 September 1841 from the notebook Branwell kept at Luddenden Foot. Below the fighters is a verse from the draft of his poem 'Lord Nelson', which was finally called 'The Triumph of Mind over Body'.*

sickle side: their brother's fits of fury and frustration, his melancholic self-pity induced by remorse and an excess of gin and opium which he cadged money from anyone he could to indulge in, grew worse after his return from Thorp Green, when he often lay around the Parsonage for hours in a drunken stupor, or raged at his unfortunate siblings.

Charlotte, the most sociably inclined of the Brontës, was mortified. In the circumstances, there was no way she could invite visitors to the house, not Ellen, nor Miss Wooler, and certainly not any well-brought-up young ladies, potential pupils for the school she had schemed of starting with Emily and Anne.

All ideas about the future seemed to have run into the sand. The three sisters had failed to some degree as governesses, and had certainly experienced great unhappiness in their ventures into the world; their salvation – a school of their own – had met with little success despite the preparations they had made and the prospectus they had issued; and now it was obvious that Branwell would never shoulder financial – or any other sort – of responsibility for the family. Charlotte described to Ellen how things were in the dreary months of 1845:

> I CAN HARDLY TELL YOU how time gets on at Haworth. There is no event whatever to mark its progress – one day resembles another – and all have heavy lifeless physiognomies – Sunday – baking-day and Saturday are the only ones that bear the slightest distinctive mark – meantime time wears away. I shall soon be thirty, and I have done nothing yet. Sometimes I get melancholy – at the prospect before and behind me … There was a time when Haworth was a very pleasant place to me, it is not so now. I feel as if we were all buried here – I long to travel, to work, to live a life of action.

1846 was to bring 'a prospect' which neither Charlotte, Emily nor Anne, had dared to contemplate.

CHAPTER 5
CURRER, ELLIS and ACTON BELL

'I ACCIDENTALLY ALIGHTED on a MS volume of verse in my sister Emily's handwriting,' wrote Charlotte recalling the autumn of 1845. 'Of course, I was not surprised, knowing that she could and did write verse: I looked it over, and something more than surprise seized me – a deep conviction that these were not common effusions nor at all like the poetry women generally write … To my ear they also had a peculiar music – wild, melancholy and elevating … The pieces are short, but they are very genuine; they stirred my heart like the sound of a trumpet when I read them alone and in secret.' The way forward seemed clear:

> WE HAD VERY EARLY cherished the dream of one day becoming authors. This dream, never relinquished even when distance divided and absorbing tasks occupied us, now suddenly acquired strength and consistency: it took the character of a resolve. We agreed to arrange a small selection of our poems, and, if possible, get them printed.

But this was by no means straightforward, for:

> MY SISTER EMILY was not a person of demonstrative character, nor one, on the recesses of whose mind and feelings, even those nearest and dearest to her could, with impunity, intrude, unlicensed; it took hours to reconcile her to the discovery I had made, and days to persuade her that such poems merited publication …

> By dint of entreaty or reason I at last wrung out the consent to have the 'rhymes' as they were contemptuously termed, published … I know no woman that ever lived ever wrote such poetry before. Condensed energy, clearness, finish – strange, strong pathos are their characteristics; utterly different from the weak diffusiveness, the laboured yet most feeble wordiness, which dilute the writings of even very popular poetesses.

OPPOSITE The Travelling Companion *by Augustus Egg (1816–63). In England in the 1840s there was talk of 'railway mania', for between 1844 and 1847 442 railways acts were passed by parliament and more than 2,000 miles of track were opened. It was an even bigger economic – and certainly social – change than the great 'canal mania' of the 1790s. The railways impinged on the lives of the Brontës in many ways: Branwell was employed by the Leeds–Manchester Railway Company; Charlotte, Emily and Anne invested their inheritance from their Aunt Branwell in railway shares, and Charlotte – and, on one occasion, Anne – would make journeys to London by train, clattering along at a speedy fifty miles an hour and getting a hitherto unseen view of life 'on the other side of the tracks'.*

This is a verdict with which subsequent critics have agreed, placing Emily Brontë among the finest and most powerful of nineteenth-century poets. But it was not just Emily's writing that Charlotte had intentions for: her plan was to publish a collection of the three sisters' poems, in the event some twenty each, for:

MEANTIME, MY YOUNGER SISTER quietly produced some of her own compositions, intimating that since Emily's had given me pleasure, I might like to look at hers. I could not but be a partial judge, yet I thought that these verses too had a sweet sincere pathos of their own.

That autumn the sisters set about making a selection of the poems to be included, discussing and editing their own and each others' work and making a fair copy. Charlotte recorded:

THE BRINGING OUT of our little book was hard work. As was to be expected, neither we nor our poems were at all wanted; but for this we had been prepared at the outset; though inexperienced ourselves, we had read the experience of others. The great puzzle lay in the difficulty of getting answers of any kind from publishers.

And there was not always harmony in the Parsonage, as Anne recalls in a poem later published under the title 'Domestic Peace', written on Monday night, 11 May 1846:

WHY SHOULD SUCH gloomy silence reign;
And why is all the house so drear,
When neither danger, sickness, pain,
Nor death, nor want have entered here?

We are as many as we were
That other night, when all were gay,
And full of hope, and free from care;
Yet, is there something gone away ...

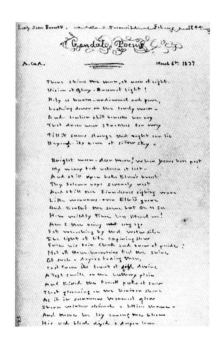

ABOVE *The first page of Emily Brontë's 'Gondal Poems' manuscript book. Gondal was the imaginary land that Emily and Anne created when they seceded from the Great Glass Town Confederacy in 1832. The prose from Gondal has been lost, but many of the poems have survived. Emily wrote Gondal poems until the end of her life, and in many of them life in Gondal is as real as life in Haworth.*

Each feels the bliss of all destroyed
And mourns the change – but each apart.

The fire is burning in the grate
As redly as it used to burn,
But still the hearth is desolate
Till Mirth and Love with Peace returns ...

But finally the publishers Aylott and Jones agreed to publish the poems, at the authors' expense, and Charlotte conducted the negotiations, specifying paper and type size. She identified the authors – up to a point:

> YOU WILL PERCEIVE that the Poems are the work of three persons – relatives – their separate pieces are distinguished by their respective signatures.

The poems were published at the end of May 1846 priced at '5s or if you think that too much for the size of the volume – say 4s.' The title page read: *Poems by Currer, Ellis and Acton Bell*. Charlotte explained that:

> AVERSE TO PERSONAL PUBLICITY, we veiled our own names under those of Currer [Charlotte], Ellis [Emily] and Acton [Anne] Bell: the ambiguous choice being dictated by a sort of conscientious scruple at assuming Christian names positively masculine, while we did not like to declare ourselves women, because – without at that time suspecting that our mode of writing and thinking was not what is called 'feminine' – we had a vague impression that authoresses are liable to be looked on with prejudice; we had noticed how critics sometimes use for their chastisement the weapon of personality, and for their reward, a flattery, which is not true praise.

ABOVE *Emily Brontë's rosewood writing desk in which an envelope from her publisher, T. C. Newby, was found, which suggests that she may have begun to write a second novel when she died.*

The *Poems* were not a commercial success – only two copies were sold of a probable print run of 1,000 – and they received but three of the 'notices in periodicals' which Charlotte had so hoped for. But at least the *Critic* review was acclamatory:

> IT IS A LONG TIME since we have enjoyed a volume of such genuine poetry as this. Amid the heaps of trash and trumpery in the shape of verses which lumber the table of the literary journalist, this small book of some 170 pages only has come like a ray of sunshine, gladdening the eye with present glory and the heart with promise of bright hours in store.

The *Athenaeum* perceptively remarked that here was 'a family in whom appears to run the instinct of song,' and Ellis [Emily] was singled out as rising:

> INTO AN INSPIRATION, which may yet find an audience in the outer world. A fine quaint spirit … which may have things to speak that men will be glad to hear, and an evident power of wing that may reach heights not here attempted.

Acton's [Anne's] poems, however, required the 'indulgence of affection', whilst Currer's [Charlotte's] were 'halfway betwixt the level of Acton's and the elevation of Ellis.' But Currer,

OPPOSITE *The Governess by Emily Osborne (1834–95). In 1848 Charlotte wrote to William Smith Williams, the reader at her publishers, offering advice about his daughter's choice of career: 'She may earn, and doubly earn her scanty salary as a daily governess. As a school-teacher she may succeed; but as a resident governess she will never (except under peculiar and exceptional circumstances) be happy … Many a time … she will wish herself a housemaid, or kitchen girl, rather than a baited, trampled, desolate, distracted governess.' Charlotte spoke from bitter experience. But never again did she have to consider that the only career open to her was that of a governess: now she was able to make literature the 'business of her life'.*

Acton and Ellis were not discouraged. Charlotte was later to recall, 'Ill-success failed to crush us … the mere effort to succeed had given a wonderful zest to existence, it must be pursued …'

Before the reviews had appeared the Brontës had already embarked on their next – and most significant – literary venture. Charlotte had written to Aylott and Jones in April, informing them that:

C.E. & A. BELL are now preparing for the Press a work of fiction, consisting of three distinct and unconnected tales which may be published either together as a work of 3 vols … or separately as single vols. as shall be deemed most advisable.

It is not their intention to publish these tales on their own account …

These 'works of fiction' were *The Professor* written by Charlotte, Emily's *Wuthering Heights* and a novel by Anne, *Agnes Grey*. Since they did not publish fiction of this sort, Messrs Aylott and Jones became the first of a long line of publishers to pass up the opportunity of publishing some of the finest writing in English literature. Charlotte realized:

IT IS EVIDENT that unknown authors have great difficulties to contend with, before they can succeed in bringing their works before the public …

These MSS. were perseveringly obtruded upon various publishers for the space of a year and a half; usually their fate was an ignominious and abrupt dismissal.

At last *Wuthering Heights* and *Agnes Grey* were accepted on terms somewhat impoverishing to the two authors; Currer Bell's book found acceptance nowhere; nor any acknowledgement of merit, so that something like the chill of despair began to invade his heart. As a forlorn hope, he tried one publishing house more – Messrs Smith and Elder.

Whilst Smith and Elder turned down *The Professor*, they wrote an encouraging rejection letter intimating that 'a work in three volumes would meet with careful attention.' And it so happened that, 'I was just then completing *Jane Eyre*, at which I had been working while the one volume tale was plodding its weary round in London …'

Charlotte had started *Jane Eyre* in the summer of 1846. On 19 August she had again taken her sixty-nine-year-old father to Manchester where Patrick, who was by now almost blind, had an appointment with William James Wilson, an eye surgeon. She wrote to Ellen:

LEFT *A portrait medallion of Branwell Brontë, cast in 1845 by the Halifax sculptor J. B. Leyland, which was described by Leyland's brother and Branwell's biographer, the noted antiquarian, Francis, as 'a life-sized medallion … in very high relief and the likeness was perfect'.*

HE PRONOUNCED PAPA'S EYES quite ready for an operation and has fixed next Monday for the performance of it – Think of us on that day dear Nell.

We got into our lodgings yesterday – I think we shall be comfortable, at least our rooms are very good … – we board ourselves – I find myself excessively ignorant – I can't tell what the deuce to order in the way of meat – &c … For ourselves I could contrive – papa's diet is so very simple – but there will be a nurse coming in a day or two – and I am afraid of not having things good enough for her – Papa requires nothing you know but plain beef and mutton, tea and bread and butter but a nurse will probably expect to live much better – give me some hints if you can –

Mr Wilson says we shall have to stay here for a month at least – it will be dreary – I wonder how poor Emily and Anne will get on at home with Branwell – they too will have their troubles – What would I not give to have you here.

It was a difficult time for Charlotte. She had 'a series of tooth-aches, prolonged and severe, bothering me both day and night,

[which] have kept me very stupid of late.' She was worried about her father and her concern about Branwell – and his effect on the family – was acute:

> **WE, I AM SORRY TO SAY,** have been somewhat more harassed than usual lately. The death of Mr Robinson, which took place about three weeks or a month ago, served Branwell for a pretext to throw all about him into hubbub and confusion with his emotions, etc., etc. Shortly after, came news from all hands that Mr Robinson had altered his will before he died and effectually prevented all chance of a marriage between his widow and Branwell, by stipulating that she should not have a shilling if she ever ventured to reopen any communication with him. Of course, he then became intolerable.
> To papa, he allows rest neither day nor night, and he is continually screwing money out of him, sometimes threatening that he will kill himself if it is withheld from him … Branwell declares that he neither can nor will do anything for himself; good situations have been offered him more than once, for which, by a fortnight's work, he might have qualified himself, but he will do nothing, except drink and make us all wretched.

Yet sitting quietly in the darkened room of the lodgings they had taken in the Oxford Road whilst Patrick convalesced after the successful removal of his cataract, Charlotte began to write quickly, in a small, slanted hand, her novel in three volumes.

Jane Eyre is the tale of the education and moral progress of the orphan Jane Eyre, and her constant crusade against petty cruelties, snobberies and hypocrisies, as she journeys from one home, and stage in life, to the next. It tells of Jane's love for the enigmatic, masterful Mr Rochester, a man she can only ultimately marry when his mutilation brings them to a state of parity. Jane demands of Mr Rochester:

> **DO YOU THINK THAT BECAUSE I AM POOR,** obscure, plain and little, I am heartless and soulless? You think wrong! I have as much soul as you – and full as much heart! And if God had gifted me with some beauty and much wealth, I should have

ABOVE *The first page of the manuscript of* Jane Eyre, *handwritten by Charlotte Brontë. She had started writing in Manchester in August 1846 and the book was eventually published by Smith, Elder & Co. in October 1847.*

OPPOSITE *An illustration of Thornfield Hall by E. M. Wimperis for an edition of* Jane Eyre. *Charlotte probably based Thornfield Hall on Ellen Nussey's home, the Rydings, a detached, castellated house at Birstall, which Branwell pronounced 'paradise' when he first visited it.*

made it as hard for you to leave me, as it now is for me to leave you. I am not talking to you through the medium of custom, conventionalities, nor even of mortal flesh: it is my spirit that addresses your spirit; just as if both had passed through the grave, and we stood at God's feet, equal – as we are!

Jane Eyre is portrayed 'as plain and as small' as Charlotte, for she wanted to prove to her sisters that a heroine could be interesting without being beautiful, though she insisted that 'she is not myself any further than that.' And though the book has a far wider compass than Charlotte's own restricted life, it draws directly on some of her own experiences and feelings, and gives meaning to others.

Charlotte despatched the completed manuscript to Smith, Elder & Co. on 24 August 1847. George Smith read it that Sunday. He was so engaged by the story that he read it at a sitting, pausing only for a glass of wine and a sandwich for lunch, cancelling an afternoon's riding engagement, bolting his dinner, and refusing to go to bed until he had finished reading it. Six weeks later, on 16 October 1847, *Jane Eyre: An Autobiography*, edited by Currer Bell, was published.

Emily and Anne, despite having had their books accepted first, were not so lucky in T. C. Newby, the first publisher of Trollope, who, in turning down *The Professor*, had agreed to publish *Agnes Grey* and *Wuthering Heights* with a subvention of £50 for an edition of 300 copies, the money refunded when 250 copies had been sold – scarcely better terms than Aylott and Jones had allowed for the Bells' *Poems*. It was not until mid-December that the claret-coloured cloth edition appeared with *Wuthering Heights*

LEFT *George Henry Lewes, the critic and essayist, who reviewed* Jane Eyre *for Fraser's Magazine. When Charlotte saw 'the aspect of Lewes' face [it] almost moved me to tears – it is so wonderfully like Emily', though the poet Swinburne hoped that Charlotte's 'bad eyesight must have misled her when she fancied a likeness between her sister and G. H. Lewes. I only met him once, but I remember … that he was the ugliest of human beings I ever saw, except perhaps his consort George Eliot.' Lewes was less affected by Charlotte, whom he described as 'a little plain, provincial, sickly-looking old maid'.*

BELOW *William Makepeace Thackeray, the author of* Vanity Fair, *who greatly admired* Jane Eyre. *Charlotte admired him – until they met, at the house of Charlotte's publisher, George Smith: 'The truth is, Charlotte Brontë's heroics roused Thackeray's antagonism. He declined to pose on a pedestal for her imagination, and with characteristic contrariety of nature he seemed to be tempted to say the very things that … affronted all her ideals … Miss Brontë wanted to persuade him that he was a great man with a "mission"; and Thackeray, with many wicked jests, declined to recognise the "mission". But, despite all this, Charlotte Brontë … never doubted his greatness. He was, she once said, "a Titan in mind".'*

and *Agnes Grey* bound together. Even then, as Charlotte wrote to her publishers:

> THE BOOKS ARE NOT well got up – they abound in errors of the press …
> I feel painfully that Ellis and Acton have not had the justice at Newby's hand
> that I have had at those of Smith and Elder.

Jane Eyre was an instant success – which no doubt is what galvanized Newby into publishing Emily and Anne's novels. William Makepeace Thackeray, the author of *Vanity Fair*, wrote to George Smith:

> I WISH YOU HAD NOT sent me *Jane Eyre*. It interested me so much that I have lost
> (or won if you like) a whole day in reading it at the busiest period with the printers
> I know wailing for copy. Who the author can be I can't guess, if a woman she knows
> her language better than most ladies do, or has had a 'classical education'. It is a
> fine book … some of the love passages made me cry, to the astonishment of John,
> who came in with the coals … I don't know why I tell you this but I have been
> exceedingly moved and pleased by *Jane Eyre*. It is a woman's writing, but whose?
> Give my respects and thanks to the author, whose novel is the first English one (and
> the French are only romances now) that I've been able to read for many a day.

George Henry Lewes, the critic soon to be notorious as the lover of George Eliot, declared *Jane Eyre* to be 'decidedly the best novel of the season' and demanded to be put directly in touch with the talented Currer Bell, which was the start of many exchanges of letters and meetings between the two. The review in *The Atlas* called it:

> ONE OF THE MOST POWERFUL domestic romances which has been published for
> many years … it is full of youthful vigour, of freshness and originality, of nervous
> diction and concentrated interest … It is a book to make the pulses gallop and the
> heart beat, and to fill the eyes with tears.

Even those reviews that were less than paeans spoke of an importance and profundity which indicated the novel's future status as a classic. The *Dublin Review* pronounced the book unsuitable for children, but recognized that Currer Bell had 'originated a new style of novel-writing'. *The Sunday Times* charged that passages between Mr Rochester and his wife were too disgusting to quote and paid Currer Bell the unintended compliment that as a writer he was never content until he had 'passed the outworks of critical reserve'.

However, *Agnes Grey* and *Wuthering Heights* found a less enthusiastic reception. *Agnes Grey*, which had been drafted under the title *Passages in the Life of an Individual*, is the story of a governess; it draws on Anne's experience with the Blakes of Mirfield Hall and the Robinsons at Thorp Green. *Douglas Jerrold's Weekly* wrote:

> WE DO NOT ACTUALLY ASSERT that the author must have been a governess himself, to describe as he does the minute torments and incessant tediums of her life, but he must have bribed some governess very largely either with love or money, to reveal to him the secrets of her prison-house, or, he must have devoted extraordinary powers of observation and discovery to the elucidation of the subject.

Although its authenticity was recognized – as Charlotte wrote the week after publication 'Agnes Grey is the mirror of the mind of the writer' – Anne ruefully remarked that the book was criticized for, 'extravagant over-colouring in those very parts that were carefully copied from the life, with a most scrupulous avoidance of exaggeration.' But on the whole, the reception was lukewarm. An unsigned review in *The Atlas* criticizes that the:

> WANT OF DISTINCTNESS in the character of Agnes … prevents the reader from taking much interest in her fate … it leaves no painful impression on the mind – some may think it leaves no impression at all.

Naturally, since they were published in the same volume, the work of Acton

ABOVE *A sketch of a cottage by Branwell Brontë, 1 July 1833. Branwell had been 'his father's and sisters' pride and hope in boyhood' and he was encouraged to pursue his artistic talent. William Robinson, his tutor, was paid two guineas an hour, which must have posed a great burden on the Brontë family finances as Patrick's annual stipend amounted to only £200. Martha, their servant, was paid just £10 per year. Whilst this drawing of a moorland cottage might have been used to illustrate one of his sisters' novels, this was not the case. Branwell seems to have been unaware of the literary production of Charlotte, Emily and Anne: according to Charlotte, 'my unhappy brother never knew what his sisters had done in literature – he was not aware that we had ever published a line.'*

BELOW *In 1872 George Smith wrote to Ellen Nussey: 'Being desirous of illustrating the works of your friend ... and her sisters with views of the scenery and places depicted in their stories, I have commissioned a skilful artist [E. M. Wimperis] to visit Haworth and its neighbourhood and make drawings ... you may possibly know the real names of some of the places so vividly described in "Jane Eyre", "Shirley" and "Wuthering Heights".'*

and Ellis Bell was compared, and *Wuthering Heights* received a baffled and often hostile press:

THE CHARACTERS ARE DRAWN from the very lowest of life; that they are inhabitants of an isolated and uncivilized district, or that they are of some demonic influence [is plain].

So wrote the critic of the *Britannia*, whilst in the opinion of the reviewer of *Douglas Jerrold's Weekly*:

THE READER IS SHOCKED, disgusted, almost sickened by details of cruelty, inhumanity, and the most diabolical hate and vengeance, and anon come passages of powerful testimony to the supreme power of love – even over demons in the human form.

Nearly all the reviews stressed the power of the narrative, its 'savage grandeur', and one was sufficiently perceptive 'to trust an author who goes at once fearlessly into the moors and desolate places for his heroes' – and, he could have added, makes those moors not simply the setting and backdrop of the book, but an actor in the drama, as Charlotte wrote in her preface to a later edition:

WITH REGARD TO THE RUSTICITY of 'Wuthering Heights,' I admit the charge, for I feel the quality. It is rustic all through. It is moorish, and wild, and knotty as a root of heath. Nor was it natural that it should be otherwise; the author being herself a native and nursling of the moors ... Ellis Bell did not describe as one whose eye and taste alone found pleasure in the prospect; her native hills were far more to her than a spectacle; they were what she lived in, and by, as much as the wild birds, their tenants, or as the heather, their produce. Her descriptions, then, of natural scenery, are what they should be, and all they should be.

Where delineation of human character is concerned, the case is different. I am bound to avow that she had scarcely more practical knowledge of the peasantry amongst whom she lived, than a nun has of the country people who sometimes pass her convent gates. My sister's disposition was not naturally gregarious; circumstances favoured and fostered her tendency to seclusion; except to go to church or take a walk on the hills, she rarely crossed the threshold of home. Though her feeling for the people round was benevolent, intercourse with them she never sought; nor, with very few exceptions, ever experienced. And yet she knew them: knew their ways, their language, their family histories; she could hear of them with interest, and talk of them with detail, minute, graphic, and accurate; but with them, she rarely exchanged a word. Hence it ensued that what her mind had gathered of the real concerning them, was too exclusively confined to those tragic and terrible traits of which, in listening to the secret annals of every rude vicinage, the memory is sometimes compelled to receive the impress. Her imagination, which was a spirit more sombre than sunny, more powerful than sportive, found in such traits material whence it wrought creations like Heathcliff, like Earnshaw, like Catherine.

Charlotte was anxious about the effect that the reviews might have on Emily, as she told Mrs Gaskell later:

> BUT EMILY – POOR EMILY – the pangs of disappointment as review after review came out about *Wuthering Heights* were terrible. Miss B. said she had no recollection of pleasure or gladness about *Jane Eyre* – every feeling was lost in seeing Emily's resolute endurance, yet knowing what she felt.

Without comment, Emily cut out five of the longest reviews and folded them carefully away in her writing desk drawer where they were discovered after her death.

Though the critics had vociferous views on the writings – and identities – of Currer, Ellis and Acton Bell, their family and friends had no idea that this androgynous trio of writers existed in their midst. It was a long time before

BELOW *William Smith Williams, 'a pale, mild, stooping man of fifty', was the reader at the publishers Smith, Elder & Co. Charlotte thought him 'so quiet, but so sincere in his attentions … most gentlemanly and well-informed.'*

Charlotte told her friend, Ellen Nussey, about the writing or publication of *Jane Eyre* and she even declined to discuss the merits of the book when Ellen unknowingly mentioned it: Branwell died without, Charlotte told her publishers, 'ever knowing that his sisters had published a line' and it was not until January 1848, when Charlotte saw an elderly clergyman reading *Jane Eyre* in Haworth, that the sisters decided that Patrick must be told. Mrs Gaskell tells the story:

> SHE [CHARLOTTE] INFORMED ME that something like the following conversation took place between her and him. (I wrote down her words the day after I heard them; and I am pretty sure they are quite accurate).
>
> 'Papa, I've been writing a book.'
> 'Have you, my dear?'
> 'Yes, and I want you to read it.'
> 'I am afraid it will try my eyes too much.'
> 'But it is not in manuscript; it is printed.'
> 'My dear! you've never thought of the expense it will be! It will be almost sure to be a loss, for how can you get a book sold? No one knows your name.'
> 'But, papa, I don't think it will be a loss; no more will you if you will just let me read you a review or two, and let me tell you more about it.'
>
> So she sat down and read some of the reviews to her father; and then, giving him a copy of 'Jane Eyre' that she intended for him, she left him to read it. When he came in to tea, he said, 'Girls, do you know Charlotte has been writing a book, and it is much better than likely?'

Charlotte's publisher began to urge the Bells to pay a visit to London and be introduced to the metropolitan *literati* who were so intrigued by their authorship. But Charlotte had to decline in February 1848:

ABOVE *The Leeds–Manchester railway, which was to be the starting point of Charlotte and Anne's dramatic trip to London to correct the 'lie' that T. C. Newby, publisher of Anne's* Agnes Grey *and Emily's* Wuthering Heights, *was perpetuating by 'affirming' to an American publisher 'that to the best of his belief "Jane Eyre", "Wuthering Heights", "Agnes Grey", and "The Tenant of Wildfell Hall" … were all the production of one author', despite having 'been told repeatedly that they were the production of three different authors'. The matter had to be sorted out, so on 7 July 1848 Charlotte and Anne 'walked through a thunderstorm to the Station, got to Leeds, and whirled up by the Night train to London'.*

I SHOULD MUCH – very much – like to take that quiet view of the 'great world' you allude to, but I have as yet won no right to give myself such a treat: it must be for some future day – when, I don't know. Ellis … would soon turn aside from the spectacle in disgust. I do not think he admits it as his creed that 'the proper study of mankind is man' – at least not the artificial man of cities.

That 'future day' was not long in coming. On 22 June 1848, Charlotte wrote again to Mr Williams:

YOU WILL PERHAPS have observed that Mr Newby has announced a new work by Acton Bell. The advertisement has, as usual, a certain tricky turn in its wording which I do not admire.

Anne, having declined Charlotte's suggestion that she and Emily should leave the unsatisfactory publishers of their first books and come under the umbrella of Smith, Elder & Co., submitted her second novel, *The Tenant of Wildfell Hall*, which was published in July. Ever since the success of *Jane Eyre*, Newby had tried to deceive the public into believing that the three Bells were in fact one: the best-selling Currer. Charlotte had reacted by issuing a disclaimer in the third edition of *Jane Eyre* when it was published in April 1848:

MY CLAIM TO THE TITLE of novelist rests on this one work alone; if, therefore, the authorship of other works of fiction has been attributed to me, an honour is awarded where it is not merited: and consequently, denied where it is justly due. This explanation will serve to rectify mistakes which may already have been made, and prevent further errors.

Newby's 'further error' was to sell *The Tenant of Wildfell Hall* to the American firm of Harper Bros. as Currer Bell's new novel. When Smith, Elder wrote to Charlotte requesting clarification, she decided that matters must be sorted out, that Smith must be presented with concrete evidence of multiple authors and the

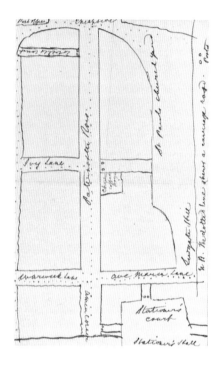

ABOVE *When Patrick Brontë came to London for his ordination in 1806, he stayed at the Chapter Coffee House in Paternoster Row near St Paul's. So when, forty years later, his daughters Charlotte and Anne ventured to London alone, their father drew them a careful map showing its location.*

BELOW *A view of Cornhill showing the houses and businesses along each side, from* London Street Views, *intending to assist strangers visiting the Metropolis through all its mazes by John Tallis (1838–40). When Charlotte and Anne visited Smith, Elder & Co., they found number 65, where the publishing house had its premises, 'to be a large bookseller's shop, in a street almost as bustling as the Strand'.*

'shuffling scamp' Newby confronted with his 'lie'. Charlotte wrote to her friend Mary Taylor, now in Wellington, New Zealand, whom she had told about her writings, and to whom she sent a copy of *Jane Eyre*, telling her about the visit.

ON THE VERY DAY I received Smith and Elder's letter – Anne and I packed up a small box, sent it down to Keighley – set out ourselves after tea – walked through a thunderstorm to the Station, got to Leeds and whirled up by the Night train to London – with the view of proving our separate identity to Smith and Elder and confronting Newby with his lie –

We arrived at the Chapter Coffee House – (our old place Polly [Mary's nickname] – we did not well know where else to go) about eight o'clock in the morning – we washed ourselves, had some breakfast, sat a few minutes and then set off in queer, inward excitement, to 65 Cornhill. Neither Mr Smith nor Mr Williams knew we were coming they had never – seen us – they did not know whether we were men or women – but had always written to us as men.

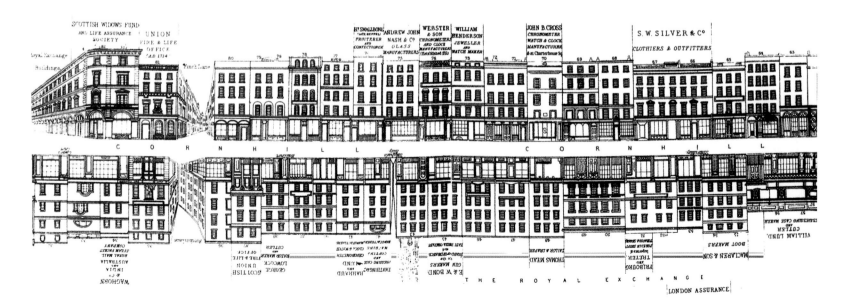

We found 65 – to be a large bookseller's shop in a street almost as bustling as the Strand – we went in – walked up to the counter – there were a great many young men and lads here and there – I said to the first I could accost – 'May I see Mr Smith – ?' he hesitated, looked a little surprised – but went to fetch him – We sat down and waited awhile – looking at some books on the counter – publications of theirs well known to us – of many of which they had sent us copies as presents. At last somebody came up and said dubiously 'Did you wish to see me, Madam?' 'Is it Mr Smith?' I said looking up through my spectacles at a young, tall, gentlemanly man 'It is.'

That first meeting made a great impression on George Smith as well:

THAT PARTICULAR SATURDAY MORNING I was at work in my room, when a clerk reported that two ladies wished to see me. I was very busy, and sent out to ask their names. The clerk returned to say that the ladies declined to give their names, but wished to see me on a private matter … I told him to show them in … two rather quaintly-dressed little ladies, pale-faced and anxious-looking, walked into my room; one of them came forward and presented me with a letter addressed in my own handwriting to 'Currer Bell, Esq.' I noticed that the letter had been opened, and said, with some sharpness, 'Where did you get this from?' 'From the post-office,' was the reply; 'it was addressed to me. We have both come that you might have ocular proof that there are at least two of us.'

Charlotte continued the narrative in her letter to Mary:

THEN [MR SMITH] said we must come and stay at his house – but we were not prepared for a long stay and declined this also – as we took our leave – he told us he should bring his sisters to call on us that evening – We returned to our Inn – and I paid for the excitement of the interview by a thundering head-ache and harassing sickness – towards evening as I got no better and expected the Smiths to call I took a strong dose of sal volatile – it roused me a little – still I was in grievous bodily case when they were announced – they came in two elegant, young ladies in full dress – prepared for the Opera – Smith himself in evening costume white gloves etc.

ABOVE *The signatures which Charlotte (Currer), Emily (Ellis) and Anne (Acton) used to disguise their identities as authors, an anonymity which they all – Emily in particular – guarded fiercely, if ineffectively.*

RIGHT *Rochester and Jane Eyre, a painting by Frederick Walter (1840–75). When Jane Eyre (seen here with her charge, Mr Rochester's fillette, Adèle) first meets the man she calls 'master', she describes him as 'of middle height, and considerable breadth of chest. He had a dark face, with stern features and a heavy brow; his eyes and gathered eyebrows looked ireful and thwarted just now; he was past youth but had not reached middle age; perhaps he might be thirty-five. I felt no fear of him, and but little shyness.'*

a distinguished, handsome fellow enough – We had by no means understood that it was settled that we were to go to the Opera – and were not ready – Moreover we had no fine, elegant dresses either with us or in the world. However on brief rumination, I thought it would be wise to make no objections – I put my headache in my pocket – we attired ourselves in the plain, high-made, country garments we possessed – and went with them to their carriage – where we found Williams likewise in full dress. They must have thought us queer, quizzical looking beings – especially me with my spectacles – I smiled inwardly at the contrast which must have been apparent between me and Mr Smith as I walked with him up the crimson carpeted staircase of the Opera House and stood amongst a brilliant throng at the box-door which was not yet open. Fine ladies and gentlemen glanced at us with a slight, graceful superciliousness quite warranted by the circumstances – Still I felt pleasurably excited – in spite of head-ache sickness and conscious clownishness, and I saw Anne was calm and gentle which she always is –

The Performance was Rossini's opera of the 'Barber of Seville' – very brilliant though I fancy there are things I should like better – We got home after one o'clock – We had never been in bed the night before – had been in constant excitement for 24 hours – you may imagine we were tired.

Enjoyable though the visit was, it exhausted Charlotte:

ON TUESDAY MORNING we left London laden with books which Mr Smith had given us, and got safely home. A more jaded wretch than I looked when I returned it would be difficult to conceive. I was thin when I went, but was meagre indeed when I returned; my face looked grey and very old, with strange, deep lines ploughed in it; my eyes stared unnaturally. I was weak and yet restless. In a while, however, the bad effects of excitement went off and I regained my normal condition.

Then there was the wrath of Emily to contend with. As she wrote to Mr Williams on her return:

OPPOSITE *The Royal Opera House, Covent Garden, where Charlotte and Anne were taken by Mr Smith of Smith, Elder & Co. and his family to see* The Barber of Seville *in July 1848. According to Mrs Gaskell, Currer and Acton Bell (a.k.a. Charlotte and Anne Brontë) became the Misses Brown for this occasion, and 'all those who came into contact with the "Miss Browns" seem only to have regarded them as shy and reserved little country-women with not much to say.' It was hardly surprising for, as Mr Williams recalled, Charlotte 'was so much struck with the architectural effect of the splendid decorations … that involuntarily she slightly pressed his arm, and whispered, "You know I am not accustomed to this sort of thing."'*

PERMIT ME TO CAUTION YOU not to speak of my sisters when you write to me. I mean, do not use the word in the plural. Ellis Bell will not endure to be alluded to under any other appellation than the *nom de plume*. I committed a grand error in betraying his identity to you and Mr Smith. It was inadvertent – the words 'we are three sisters' escaped me before I was aware. I regretted the avowal the moment I had made it; I regret it bitterly now, for I find it is against every feeling and intention of Ellis Bell.

But the separate identity and the sex of the authors had been established. The Brontë sisters were established writers: there was no more talk of governessing or having to start a school. On 4 January 1848 Charlotte had written in reply to Mr Williams' good wishes for the New Year, 'I wish you too *many, many*, happy new years, and prosperity and success to you and yours.' In midsummer that same year, it began to look as if Charlotte, Emily and Anne Brontë might themselves be laying claim to a measure of that prosperity, success and happiness in the future too.

CHAPTER 6
CHARLOTTE ALONE

'WE HAVE BURIED OUR DEAD out of sight,' Charlotte wrote to her publisher on 2 October 1848. 'A lull begins to succeed the gloomy tumult of last week. It is not permitted us to grieve for him who is gone as others grieve for those they lose. The removal of our only brother must necessarily be regarded by us rather in the light of a mercy than a chastisement. Branwell was his father's and his sisters' pride and hope in boyhood, but since manhood the case has been otherwise. It has been our lot to see him take a wrong bent; to hope, expect, wait his return to the right path … to experience despair at last – and now to behold the sudden early obscure close of what might have been a noble career.

'I do not weep from a sense of bereavement – there is no prop withdrawn, no consolation torn away, no dear companion lost – but for the wreck of talent, the ruin of promise, the untimely dreary extinction of what might have been a burning and a shining light.'

Branwell, who had long suffered from 'intolerable mental wretchedness and corporeal weakness', had in effect written his own tragic epitaph four years earlier in a poem published in the *Halifax Guardian* in May 1842, 'On Peaceful Death and Painful Life':

> *WHY DOEST THOU SORROW for the happy dead?*
> *For, if their life be lost, their toils are o'er,*
> *And woe and want can trouble them no more …*
> *So, turn from such as these thy drooping head,*
> *And mourn the Dead Alive – whose spirit flies –*
> *Whose life departs, before his death has come;*
> *Who knows no Heaven beneath life's gloomy skies*
> *Who sees no Hope to brighten up the gloom, –*
> *'Tis he who feels the worm that never dies, –*
> *The real death and darkness of the tomb.*

OPPOSITE *A Woman by the Fireside by Marcus Stone (1840–1921).* 'A year ago,' wrote Charlotte, 'had a prophet warned me how I should stand in June 1849 – how stripped and bereaved – had he foretold the autumn, the winter, the spring of sickness and suffering to be gone through – I should have thought – this can never be endured. It is over. Branwell – Emily – Anne – are gone like dreams – gone as Maria and Elizabeth went twenty years ago. One by one I have watched them fall asleep on my arm – and closed their glazed eyes – I have seen them buried one by one – and – thus far – God has upheld me. From my heart I thank Him.'

LEFT *Portrait of Charlotte by George Richmond, a gift from her publisher to her father. Patrick thanked Smith:* 'I may be partial … but I fancy I see strong indications of the genius of the author of "Shirley" and "Jane Eyre".' *In private, however, he opined that the portrait made Charlotte look older.*

'A marble calm' settled over the Parsonage. Charlotte had arranged for Smith, Elder to reissue the *Poems*, and Anne's second novel, *The Tenant of Wildfell Hall*, had been published in June to mixed reviews. An American reviewer 'gladly hail[ed]' the book as:

BOLDLY AND ELOQUENTLY developing blind places of wayward passion in the human heart, which is far more interesting to trace than all the bustling lanes and murky alleys through which the will-o'-the-wisp genius of Dickens has so long led the public mind.

OPPOSITE *An illustration by E. M. Wimperis for* The Tenant of Wildfell Hall *by Anne Brontë, published in 1848 when she was twenty-eight. Although the* Athenaeum *cited it as 'the most interesting novel we have read for a month past', charges of coarseness were levelled at it by the critics and by Charlotte. Anne wrote a vigorous defence of her novel in a preface to the second edition, but she can hardly have been surprised at its reception; in 'The Narrow Way', a poem written that April, she advised: 'Believe not those who say/The upward path is smooth,/Lest thou shouldst stumble in the way,/And faint before the truth.'*

Another charged that the:

WHOLE FIRM OF BELL & CO. seem to have a sense of depravity of human nature peculiarly their own … this is particularly the case with Acton Bell …

The book's story of two worlds, in which Helen Graham, a principled and religious girl, marries the dissolute Arthur Huntingdon, is an uncomfortable one, a saga of uncontrolled appetite and the undirected education of the wealthy – a theme Anne knew well from her days as a governess – the vulnerability of women in society and their largely unsuccessful attempts to improve the moral tone of that society. It made a demand for a re-examination of conventional views of the 'fallen woman' of Victorian morality and thus for women's sexual – and legal – equality.

Despite reviewers' charges of 'coarseness', 'brutality' and 'morbid revelling in scenes of debauchery', the book proved a *succès de scandale*, immensely popular with customers of the circulating libraries, and enjoying sales second only to *Jane Eyre*.

By the end of October, Charlotte was seriously concerned about the frailty of both her sisters. She later wrote:

MY SISTER EMILY FIRST DECLINED … She sank rapidly. She made haste to leave us. Yet, while physically she perished, mentally, she grew stronger than we had yet known her. Day by day, when I saw with what a front she met suffering, I looked on her with an anguish of wonder and love. I have seen nothing like it; but, indeed, I have never seen her parallel in anything. Stronger than a man, simpler than a child, her nature stood alone.

Emily was buried on 22 December 1848 in the vault in Haworth Church where her mother and brother lay. She was painfully thin when she died of consumption (tuberculosis). Her coffin was made by the local carpenter, William Wood: it measured her height, 5 feet 7 inches, but was only 17 inches across – the narrowest he had ever fashioned.

On Christmas Eve 1848, a week after Emily's funeral, Charlotte, who had lost 'the person who [was] closest to my heart in the world', sat down to write a lament:

> *My darling thou wilt never know*
> *The grinding agony of woe*
> *That we have borne for thee,*
> *Thus may we consolation tear*
> *E'en from the depth of our despair*
> *And wasting misery.*

In four months, Patrick Brontë had lost two children: Branwell at thirty-one, Emily at thirty. But the tragedies were not yet at an end. As Charlotte wrote to her old teacher from Roe Head, Miss Wooler:

> We saw Emily torn from the midst of us when our hearts clung to her with intense attachment … she was hardly buried when Anne's health failed – and we were warned that Consumption had found another victim in her, and it would be vain to reckon on her life.

Anne had lost her closest friend, fellow Gondal creator and diary correspondent, and now she was close to death herself. She wrote to Ellen Nussey, 'The doctors say that a change of air or removal to a better climate would hardly ever fail of success in consumptive cases,' and on 24 May 1849 Charlotte and Ellen took Anne to take the sea air at Scarborough. But in Anne's case it was too late. Charlotte wrote to William Smith, her publisher, now her friend:

> You have been informed of my dear sister Anne's death … Her quiet, Christian death did not rend my heart as Emily's stern, simple, undemonstrative end did. I let Anne go to God, and felt he had a right to her. I could hardly let Emily go. I wanted to hold her back then, and I want her back now … They are both gone, and so is poor Branwell, and Papa now has me only – the weakest, puniest, least promising

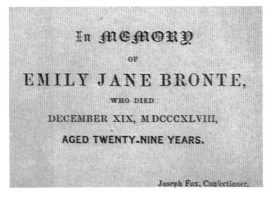

ABOVE *The memorial card of Emily Jane Brontë. In an earlier poem, she had written: 'Yes, as my swift days near their goal/Tis all that I implore –/In life and death a chainless soul,/With courage to endure!'*

RIGHT A Parody, *a sketch by Branwell of death summoning him to a fight; Haworth Church appears in the background. When he lost the fight, on 24 September 1848, he cried out to his father's sexton and his friend, John Brown: 'In all my past life I have done nothing either great or good. Oh John, I am dying!' But the epitaph of Francis Grundy, a friend from Luddenden Foot days, was more generous: 'Poor, brilliant, gay, moody, moping, wildly excitable, miserable Branwell. No history records your many struggles after the good – Your wit, brilliance, attractiveness, eagerness for excitement – all the qualities which made you such "good company" and dragged you down to such an untimely grave.'*

of his six children. Consumption has taken the whole five … Why life is so blank, brief, and bitter I do not know.

Anne was twenty-nine when she died. 'I have buried her here at Scarboro', to save Papa the anguish of the return and a third funeral,' wrote Charlotte. By the end of June, Charlotte was back at Haworth. She wrote to Mr Williams:

> I AM NOW AGAIN AT HOME where I returned last Thursday. I call it *home* still – much as London would be called London if an earthquake should shake its streets to ruins. But let me not be ungrateful: Haworth parsonage is still a home for me, and not quite a ruined or desolate home either. Papa is there – and two most affectionate and faithful servants – and two old dogs, in their way as faithful and affectionate.

Just as, as children, Charlotte, her sisters and brother had always 'made out' an imaginary 'world within' as counterbalance to the unacceptable realities of the world without, Charlotte in her intense loneliness resumed her writing. In October 1849 her second book, *Shirley*, was published. She was anxious about the book, eagerly awaited after the extraordinary success of *Jane Eyre*, and written in the most difficult of circumstances. 'Worse than useless did it seem to attempt to write what there no longer lived an "Ellis Bell" to read.' But Charlotte recognized the curative power of her writing:

> WHATEVER BECOMES OF the work, the occupation of writing has been a real boon to me. It took me out of dark and desolate reality into an unreal but happier region … imagination lifted me when I was sinking …
> I am thankful to God, who gave me this faculty.

She links this belief with the stifling effect of womanly duties in one of the most striking passages in *Shirley* when Rose Yorke (who was based on Mary Taylor) tells one of the book's two heroines, Caroline Helstone, that it is 'a sin to leave your life a blank' and not use your God-given abilities:

ABOVE *A caricature of the so-called 'Luddites', supposedly under the leadership of 'General Ludd', a Nottinghamshire weaver who tried to resist the mechanization of the textile industry by smashing machinery. The unrest spread to the woollen mills of Yorkshire and there were riots around Hartshead when Patrick Brontë was a curate there in the winter of 1811–12.*

'IF MY MASTER HAS GIVEN ME ten talents, my duty is to trade with them, and make ten talents more. Not in the dust of household drawers shall the coin be interred. I will not deposit it in a broken-spouted tea-pot, and shut it up in a china closet among tea things. I will not commit it to your work-table to be smothered in piles of woollen hose. I will not prison it in the linen press to find shrouds among the sheets: and least of all … will I hide it in a tureen of cold potatoes, to be ranged with bread, butter, pastry, and ham on the shelves of the larder.'

Shirley's eponymous central character took on many of the attributes and circumstances of Emily: 'what Emily Brontë would have been had she been placed in health and prosperity', Charlotte told Mrs Gaskell, as 'Tallii' resurrected aspects of her sister and her life. Determined to refute the criticisms of 'coarseness' which *Jane Eyre* had attracted, Charlotte intended her book to be 'as unromantic as a Monday morning' and the story links the lot of the female characters to that of the mill workers as comparable forms of oppression, and explores the antagonism between the male sphere of work and industry with the female one of nature and feeling, the tensions between which are expressed in Mr Helstone's remarks to his niece, Caroline:

'WHEN WOMEN ARE SENSIBLE – and, above all, intelligible – I can get on with them. It is only the vague, superfine sensations, and extremely wire-drawn notions, that put me about. Let a woman ask me to give her an edible or a wearable … I can at least understand the demand: but when they pine for they know not what – sympathy – sentiment – some of these infinite abstractions – I can't do it.'

ABOVE Hollow's Mill, *a drawing by E. M. Wimperis to illustrate* Shirley *(1849). Charlotte had heard her father's stories of the riots of 1811–12, during the Napoleonic wars, when the Orders in Council had had the effect of cutting off the principal markets for Yorkshire woollen goods, bringing the industry to near ruin. She drew on the Luddites' attack on Rawfolds Mill near Hartshead in writing* Shirley, *making Rawfolds Hollow's Mill: 'misery generates hate: these sufferers hated the machines which they believed took their bread from them; they hated the buildings which contained those machines; they hated the manufacturers who owned those buildings.'*

Charlotte drew a parallel between this denial of feeling with the desperate situation which drove workmen to become machine wreckers, so-called Luddites, in the winter of 1811–12, an experience which Patrick Brontë had often related from his days at Hartshead when rioters had attacked Cartwright's Mill.

It was these assigned roles that had created the 'warped system of things', perpetuating a feminine ideal for women which may neither accord with their intellectual abilities, nor often – certainly in the case of the Brontë sisters – their economic necessities; which afforded no place in society for the middle-class spinster with no proper outlet for her emotions or her energies, whose lot is repression, to 'ask no questions; utter no remonstrances … [but take the scorpion fate has offered] show no consternation: close your fingers firmly upon the gift; let it sting through your palm', and whose only hope can be subservience in marriage or service as a governess. Nor did this system recognize the worker's grievance that he is the victim of political, social and economic forces against which he has no legitimate redress.

The book's title page bore the legend: Shirley, A Tale by Currer Bell, Author of 'Jane Eyre'. Charlotte was still anxious to shield her true identity; but to no avail. Four months later she wrote to Ellen:

> MARTHA [A SERVANT AT THE PARSONAGE] came in yesterday, puffing and blowing, and much excited. 'I've heard such news,' she began. 'What about?' 'Please ma'am, you've been and written two books, the grandest books that ever was seen. My father heard it at Halifax, and Mr George Taylor and Mr Greenwood, and Mr Merrall at Bradford; and they are going to have a meeting at the Mechanics' Institute, and to settle about ordering them.' 'Hould your tongue Martha, and be off.' I fell into a cold sweat. 'Jane Eyre' will be read by John Brown, by Mrs Taylor, and Betty. God help, keep, and deliver me!

Charlotte's fame was beginning to pull her into the 'world without', not this time as a despised governess, but as a respected author. Her books were proving to be

ABOVE *'Yesterday we went to the Crystal Palace,' wrote Charlotte to her father of her visit to the Great Exhibition, which opened in Hyde Park in May 1851 and was housed in Joseph Paxton's great glass edifice. 'The exterior has a strange and elegant but somewhat unsubstantial effect. The interior is like a mighty Vanity Fair. The brightest colours blaze on all sides; and wares of all kinds, from diamonds to spinning jennies and printing presses, are there to be seen. It was very fine, gorgeous, animated, bewildering, but I liked Thackeray's lecture better.'*

BELOW *'The secretary of the Zoological Society … sent me a ticket of admission to their gardens, which I wish you could see,' wrote Charlotte to her father. 'There are animals from all parts of the world enclosed in great cages – lions, tigers, elephants, numberless monkeys … all sorts of living snakes and lizards in cages, some great Ceylon toads not much smaller than Flossy, some large foreign rats nearly as large and fierce as bull-dogs.'*

'a passport to the society of clever people' and to London; within weeks she was writing to Ellen:

> I CAME TO THIS big Babylon last Thursday, and have been in what seems to me a sort of whirl ever since, for changes, scenes, and stimulus which would be a trifle to others are much to me.

Charlotte was to pay five visits to London, and meet many of the most celebrated writers of her day. She found these trips both enjoyable and a great strain for her shy nature and delicate constitution.

Outings for Charlotte on these visits were largely arranged by her publishers. Mr Williams, who was known to work thirty-six hours at a stretch sometimes, sustained only by mutton and green tea, took time off to squire his retiring author around town. On her various visits to the metropolis she was taken to the National Gallery to see an exhibition of Turner's watercolours ('Nothing charmed me more,' she reported to Miss Wooler); the new Houses of Parliament; she saw Rossini's *Barber of Seville* at Covent Garden, and attended productions of *Macbeth* and *Othello* at the theatre. She saw the great French *tragédienne* Rachel play in *Adrienne Lecouvreur* and *Les Trois Horaces* – though not her greatest role as *Phèdre*, which she also played at St James theatre in the summer of 1851 – and was deeply affected by the performances. She saw the summer exhibition at the Royal Academy; she was taken five times to see Joseph Paxton's Crystal Palace, which housed the Great Exhibition, in Hyde Park; and had gone incognito as 'Miss Fraser' to visit a phrenologist.

But it was not only sights that Charlotte saw in London; she met more people than she had encountered in the entire rest of her life. She met Thackeray, who had been so enthusiastic about *Jane Eyre* and to whom she had dedicated the second edition – an unfortunate *faux-pas* since, like Mr Rochester, his wife was mad. Thackeray was somewhat patronizing about the provincial and shy Miss Brontë:

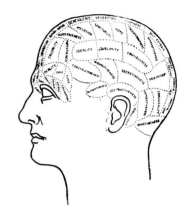

ABOVE *In June 1851 Charlotte went incognito as Miss Fraser to see a phrenologist. His conclusion was: 'Temperament for the large part nervous … In its intellectual development this head is very remarkable … this lady possesses a fine organ of language, and can, if she has done her talents justice by exercise, express her sentiments with clearness, precision, and force – sufficiently eloquent but not verbose.'*

RIGHT *The novelist Mrs Gaskell by George Richmond (1851). Charlotte met her in 1850 and found her 'a woman of many fine qualities … [She] deserves the epithet which I find is generally applied to her – charming.' When Mrs Gaskell came to write Charlotte's life, she resolved 'to put down everything I remembered about this dear friend and noble woman'.*

RIGHT *Harriet Martineau by George Richmond (1849). 'I admire her and wonder at her more than I can say,' wrote Charlotte in 1850. 'Her powers of labour, of exercise, and social cheerfulness are beyond my comprehension. In spite of the unceasing activity of her colossal intellect she enjoys good health … she must think I am a very insignificant person compared to herself.'*

I REMEMBER the trembling little frame, the little hand, the great honest eyes. An impetuous honesty seemed to me to characterise the woman … I fancied an austere little Joan of Arc marching in upon us, and rebuking our easy lives, our easy morals. She gave me the impression of being a very pure, and lofty, and high-minded person.

Charlotte was very anxious to meet the writer and political economist Harriet Martineau, and sent a note, signed 'Currer Bell' requesting a meeting. The formidable Miss Martineau recalled:

I THOUGHT HER the smallest creature I had ever seen (except at a fair) and her eyes blazed, as it seemed to me … When she was seated by me on the sofa, she cast me such a look – so loving, and so appealing – that, in connexion with her deep mourning dress, and the knowledge that she was the sole survivor of her family, I could with the utmost difficulty return her smile, or keep my composure. I should have been heartily glad to cry. We soon got on well …

In fact Harriet Martineau and Charlotte Brontë had little in common, since Miss Martineau was well educated, well travelled, well connected, confident, irreligious and committed to political pamphleteering. But the two remained friends, somewhat surprisingly, and Charlotte visited the older woman at her cottage at Ambleside in the Lake District. Their unlikely friendship came to an abrupt end, however, over Charlotte's last book *Villette*, published in 1854, when Miss Martineau complained that it represented

OPPOSITE *An illustration of Lake Windermere from Harriet Martineau's* A Complete Guide to the English Lakes. *Charlotte visited her in nearby Ambleside in 1850: 'The house is very pleasant both within and without – Her visitors enjoy the most perfect liberty; what she claims for herself she allows them. I rise at my own hour, breakfast alone – (she is up at five, takes a cold bath and a walk by starlight and has finished breakfast and got to her work by 7 o'clock).*

RIGHT *'The visit to Mrs Gaskell on my way home [from London, in June 1851],' wrote Charlotte, 'let me down easily; though I only spent two days with her they were very pleasant. She lives in a large, cheerful, airy house, quite out of Manchester smoke; a garden surrounds it, and, as in this hot weather the windows were kept open, a whispering of leaves and perfume of flowers always invaded the house … Haworth Parsonage is rather a contrast.'*

woman as seeing life only in terms of love. Charlotte felt deeply betrayed by this misreading and never saw Harriet again.

It was in the Lake District, while staying with the educational reformer Sir James Kay Shuttleworth, in 1850, that Charlotte met the person whose friendship was to be so important to her in her own lifetime and to whose intimacy with Charlotte we are indebted for our subsequent knowledge of her life: the writer Elizabeth Cleghorn Gaskell:

> FORTUNATELY THERE WAS MRS GASKELL (the authoress of 'Mary Barton')
> who came to the Briery the day after me – I was truly glad of her companionship.
> She is a woman of the most genuine talent – of cheerful, pleasing and cordial
> manners and – I believe – of a kind and good heart.

And Mrs Gaskell warmed to Charlotte, whose writing as Currer Bell had interested her since the first publication of *Jane Eyre*. The friendship was to

blossom. The two writers corresponded frequently and at the end of June 1851, Charlotte broke her return journey from London and stayed for two days with Mrs Gaskell at her home at Plymouth Grove, 'a large, cheerful, airy house quite out of the Manchester smoke'. Charlotte was greatly drawn too to the Gaskells' happy family life and grew particularly fond of the two younger daughters, Flossy and Julia; she once wrote:

COULD YOU MANAGE to convey a small kiss to that dear but dangerous little person, Julia? She surreptitiously possessed herself of a minute fraction of my heart, which has been missing ever since I saw her.

In September 1853 Mrs Gaskell paid a long-promised visit to Charlotte at Haworth. The contrast could not have been greater. At the Parsonage:

LIFE IS LIKE CLOCKWORK. No one comes to the house; nothing disturbs the deep repose; hardly a voice is heard; you catch the ticking of the clock in the kitchen, or the buzzing of a fly in the parlour all over the house. Miss Brontë sits alone in her parlour, breakfasting with her father in his study at nine o'clock. She helps in the housework; for one of their servants, Tabby, is nearly ninety, and the other only a girl. Then I accompanied her in her walks on the sweeping moors … Oh! those high, wild, desolate moors, up above the whole world, and the very realms of silence! … We have generally had another walk before tea, which is at six; at half-past eight prayers; and by nine o'clock all the household are in bed except ourselves. We sit up together till ten, or past; and after I go I hear Miss Brontë come down and walk up and down the room for an hour or so.

The time after the deaths of Branwell, Emily and Anne was one of painful loneliness, only occasionally punctuated by these excursions into the wider world which Charlotte enjoyed but also found exhausting and debilitating. The memories of Anne, and particularly Emily, were everywhere, and Charlotte found it unbearably sad to walk alone where the sisters had formerly roamed together:

I AM FREE to walk on the moors, but when I go out there alone everything reminds me of the times when others were with me, and then the moors seem a wilderness, featureless, solitary, saddening. My sister Emily had a particular love for them, and there is not a knoll of heather, nor a branch of fern, nor a young bilberry leaf, nor a fluttering lark or linnet, but reminds me of her. The distant prospects were Anne's

RIGHT *The opening page of Charlotte Brontë's manuscript of* Villette, *a book she found difficult to write. When she finally despatched the manuscript to her patient publishers, she wrote to Ellen 'truly thankful I am to be able to tell you that I finished my long task on Saturday; packed and sent off the parcel to Cornhill. I said my prayers when I had done it. Whether it is ill or well done, I don't know.'*

LEFT *Garden in the Rue Fosette, an illustration for* Villette *(1853). 'Villette' is Brussels renamed, and the experiences of Lucy Snowe at Madame Beck's Pensionnat de Demoiselles draw inspiration from the eighteen months Charlotte spent at the Pensionnat Heger in Brussels. Just as the school's garden 'had been important for Charlotte, so she made it for Lucy Snowe: 'On summer mornings I used to rise early, to enjoy [the gardens behind the house] alone; on summer evenings, to linger solitary, to keep tryst with the rising moon, or taste one kiss of the evening breeze, or fancy rather than feel the freshness of dew descending.'*

delight, and when I look round she is in the blue tints, the pale mists, the waves and shadows of the horizon. In the hill-country silence their poetry comes by lines and stanzas into my mind: once I loved it; now I dare not read it, and I am driven often to wish I could taste one draught of oblivion and forget …

During this time Charlotte was engaged in two writing projects which she found agonizingly difficult to complete. In 1850, Smith, Elder had proposed a new publication of the Brontës' writings, and Charlotte set herself to this 'exquisitely painful and depressing task'. As guardian of her sisters' reputation, she was equivocal about whether Emily and Anne had left any unpublished material that could now be included in a definitive edition: 'I would not offer a line to the publication of which my sisters themselves would have objected.' And in her very limited selection of Emily's poems, she admitted: 'I have, then, culled from the mass only a little poem here and there. The whole makes but a tiny nosegay, and the colour and perfume of the flowers are not such as fit them for festal use.'

With her conviction that the dissolute character of Arthur Huntingdon was too exact a portrait of Branwell, Charlotte was opposed to a reprint of Anne's second novel. '*Wildfell Hall* it hardly appears to me desirable to preserve,' she wrote to Mr Williams, and in deference to Charlotte's feelings, it was not reissued until after her death. But in her introduction to a new edition of *Wuthering Heights* and *Agnes Grey*, she wrote a tribute to her two sisters:

> IN EXTERNALS, THEY WERE two unobtrusive women; a perfectly secluded life gave them retiring manners and habits. In Emily's nature the extremes of vigour and simplicity seemed to meet. Under an unsophisticated culture, inartificial tastes, and an unpretending outside, lay a secret power and fire that might have informed the brain and kindled the veins of a hero; but she had no worldly wisdom; her powers were unadapted to the practical business of life … An interpreter ought always to have stood between her and the world …

Anne's character was milder and more subdued ... but was well-endowed with quiet virtues ... Neither Emily nor Anne was learned; they had no thought of filling their pitchers at the well-spring of other minds; they always wrote from the impulse of nature, the dictates of intuition, and from such stores of observation as their limited experience had enabled them to amass ... for those who had known them all their lives in the intimacy of close relationship, they were genuinely good and truly great.

But Charlotte's own next novel was causing her great difficulty. The first book to be entirely conceived without discussion with her family scribes, it dealt with a subject that was particularly painful for her. Ten years after returning from Brussels, *Villette* recreated the city and its painful associations with M. Heger, who was the model for Paul Emmanuel, the teacher of French literature.

Her patient publishers were inclined to lose heart; tiny, shy, nervous Miss Brontë did not shine in society, was never going to become either the toast of the literary salons, or a prolific writer like Thackeray or Dickens – or even like her friend, Mrs Gaskell. She would never 'make 'em laugh, make 'em wait, make 'em cry' as Wilkie Collins counselled successful authors. Charlotte wrote painfully, her productivity interrupted by spells of illness and depression. She had written sharply to Mr Williams when he suggested announcing a publication date for the new book:

> IT IS NOT AT ALL LIKELY that my book will be ready at the time you mention. If my health is spared I shall get on with it as fast as is consistent with its being done, if not well, yet as well as I can do it, not one whit faster. When the mood leaves me (it has left me now, without vouchsafing so much as a word of a message when it will return) I put by the MS. and wait till it comes back again; and God knows I sometimes have to wait long – very long it seems to me.

But finally, on 20 November 1852, three years after *Shirley* had been published, Charlotte sent off her manuscript to Smith, Elder. 'The book, I think, will not

BELOW *Charlotte's trinket box with a picture of St Gudule's Cathedral on the lid. When she was in Brussels, Charlotte 'found myself opposite Ste Gudule ... I went in, quite alone ... an odd whim came into my head ... in two confessionals I saw a priest. I felt as if I did not care what I did, provided it was not absolutely wrong, and that it served to vary my life and yield a moment's interest. I took a fancy to change myself into a Catholic and go and make a real confession to see what it was like.'*

ABOVE *Rachel is 'a wonderful sight … terrible as if the earth had cracked deep at your feet and revealed a glimpse of hell … I shall never forget it … she is not a woman – she is a snake – she is the – –. So profound an effect did the great French actress (shown here) have on Charlotte when she saw her on the London stage that she reproduced her own mesmerized fascination in Lucy Snowe's reaction to* Vashti *in* Villette.

be considered pretentious, nor is it of a character to excite hostility,' she told Ellen Nussey.

In her story of Lucy Snowe, an exploration of powerlessness and repression, and the crafting of a new identity, Charlotte had renamed not only Brussels, the city of her most profoundly felt experience with M. Heger, but had also redrawn her own understanding of the experience. In the words she gives to Lucy Snowe:

'SO THIS SUBJECT IS DONE WITH. It is right to look our life-accounts bravely in the face now and then, and settle them honestly … Call anguish – anguish, and despair – despair; write both down in strong characters with resolute pen; you will better pay your debt to Doom. Falsify; insert "privilege" where you should have written "pain" and see if your mighty creditor will allow fraud to pass, or accept the coin with which you would cheat him. Offer to the strongest – if the darkest angel of God's host – water, when he asked blood – will he take it? Not a whole pale sea for one red drop. I settled another account.'

Villette was to be Charlotte's last novel. It drew critical acclaim when it was published on 28 January 1853, and was generally regarded as 'confirmation of Currer Bell's genius'. C. H. Lewes eulogized that 'In Passion and power – those noble twins of Genius – Currer Bell has no living rival except George Sand'; while George Eliot wrote to a friend: 'Villette, Villette, – have you read it? … I am only just returning to a sense of the real world about me, for I have been reading "Villette", a still more wonderful book than "Jane Eyre". There is something preternatural in its power.'

A few weeks after the dispatch of *Villette* to her publishers, and while she waited for their response to the final volume, Charlotte wrote to Ellen about the disturbing behaviour of her father's curate, the Reverend Arthur Bell Nicholls:

ON MONDAY EVENING Mr Nicholls was here to tea. I vaguely felt without clearly seeing, as without seeing, I have felt for some time, the meaning of his constant looks and strange, feverish restraint. After tea I withdrew to the dining-room as usual. As usual, Mr Nicholls sat with papa till between eight and nine o'clock, I then heard him open the parlour door as if going. I expected the clash of the front-door. He stopped in the passage: he tapped: like lightning it flashed on me what was coming. He entered – he stood before me. What his words were you can guess; his manner – you can hardly realise – never can I forget it. Shaking from head to foot, looking deadly pale, speaking low, vehemently yet with difficulty – he made me for the first time feel what it costs a man to declare affection where he doubts response ...

When he was gone I immediately went to papa, and told him what had taken place. Agitation and anger disproportionate to the occasion ensued; if I had *loved* Mr Nicholls and had heard such epithets applied to him as were used, it would have transported me past my patience; as it was, my blood boiled with a sense of injustice, but papa worked himself into a state not to be trifled with, the veins on his face started up like whipcord, and his eyes became bloodshot. I made haste to promise that Mr Nicholls should on the morrow have a distinct refusal.

Mr Nicholls' was the fourth proposal of marriage that Charlotte had received. The first came in March 1839 from Ellen Nussey's brother, Henry, a clergyman. Charlotte had declined it at once:

MY ANSWER TO YOUR PROPOSAL must be a *decided negative* ... I have no personal repugnance to the idea of a union with you, but I feel convinced that mine is not the sort of disposition calculated to form the happiness of a man like you ... you do not know me; I am not the serious, grave, cool-headed individual you suppose; you would think me romantic and eccentric; you would say I was satirical and severe. However, I scorn deceit, and I will never, for the sake of attaining the distinction of matrimony and escaping the stigma of an old maid, take a worthy man whom I am conscious I cannot render happy.

OPPOSITE *The Reverend Patrick Brontë in old age. When Mrs Gaskell first met Patrick he was seventy-six years old. She found him a 'tall fine-looking old man, with silver bristles all over his head; nearly blind … he was very polite and agreeable to me; paying me rather elaborate, old-fashioned compliments, but I was sadly afraid of him in my inmost soul; for I caught a glare of his stern eyes over his spectacles at Miss Brontë once or twice which made me know my man; and he talked at her sometimes; he is very fearless … and is consequently much respected and to be respected. But he ought never to have married. He did not like children.'*

OPPOSITE *The Reverend Arthur Bell Nicholls, c.1854. Mrs Gaskell was 'terrified he won't let her [Charlotte] go on being intimate with us heretics … I fancy him very good, but very stern and bigoted … He sounds vehemently in love with her.'*

In August the same year 'Mr Bryce … a young Irish clergyman fresh from Dublin University' was brought by a former curate at Haworth to visit the Brontës. He and Charlotte passed a pleasant evening together, and his next communication with her was a letter proposing marriage. 'Well! thought I', she wrote to Ellen, 'I have heard of love at first sight, but this beats all.'

The third proposal came in April 1851, when James Taylor, who worked for Charlotte's publishers, called at the Parsonage on his way back from a trip to Scotland. Mr Taylor was bound for India, where he was to man the Smith, Elder offices, and he proposed that Charlotte should accompany him as his wife. Again she declined. Despite her admission that 'I feel to my deep sorrow – to my humiliation – that it is not in my power to bear the canker of constant solitude,' Charlotte was soberly realistic about her expectations:

> NOT THAT IT IS A CRIME to wish to marry, or a crime to wish to be married; but it is an imbecility, which I reject with contempt, for women, who have neither fortune nor beauty, to make marriage the principal object of their wishes and hopes, and the aim of all their actions; not to be able to convince themselves that they are unattractive, and that they had better be quiet, and think of things other.

Arthur Nicholls could not 'think of things other', and from his curacy at Kirk Smeaton near Pontefract, he wrote to Charlotte – six times before she permitted herself a reply 'exhorting him to heroic submission to his lot'. The correspondence continued in secret until Charlotte, troubled by the deceit, persuaded her father that she should get to know his ex-curate better and explore her own feelings towards him. This slow attrition was successful and on 11 April 1854 Charlotte wrote to Ellen:

> MR NICHOLLS HAS PERSEVERED … certainly I must respect him, nor can I withhold from him more than mere cool respect. In fact, dear Ellen, I am engaged.

LEFT *The now faded lavender and silver striped silk dress that Charlotte wore when she went off on her honeymoon. Her publisher later commented on the very small waist: 'it shocks the natural respect for a fine genius to say it; but I have no doubt that tight-lacing shortened Charlotte Brontë's life.'*

BELOW *A photograph of Charlotte, probably taken on her honeymoon in 1854. It was only discovered in 1984, and is flattering in that Charlotte does not here seem to match Mrs Gaskell's description of someone who was* 'under-developed … altogether *plain'.*

OPPOSITE *The Gap of Dunloe, which Charlotte and Arthur Nicholls visited on their honeymoon, and where 'the glimpse of a very grim phantom … came on' when Charlotte was thrown from her horse and was in danger of being trampled to death, until she was finally rescued 'neither bruised by the fall nor touched by the mare's hoofs'.*

Mr Nicholls … will return to the curacy of Haworth. I stipulated that I would not leave Papa, and to Papa himself I proposed a plan of residence which should maintain his seclusion and convenience uninvaded and in a pecuniary sense bring him gain instead of loss.

At eight o'clock in the morning of Thursday 29 June 1854 Charlotte Brontë married the Reverend Arthur Bell Nicholls at Haworth church with 'reasonable expectations of happiness'. Patrick Brontë was not present: the bride was given in marriage by Miss Wooler, her old teacher from Roe Head.

Her 'reasonable expectations' seem to have been reasonably fulfilled. The Nicholls honeymooned in Ireland, home of both their ancestors, but Charlotte's first visit. They visited Cuba Court, just outside Banagher, where Arthur had been brought up by his uncle, Dr Bell. It was an imposing residence and Charlotte was impressed, as she was by the 'English manners' of her Celtic in-laws.

But the long shadow of the Parsonage and her ailing father fell across their expedition. Little more than three weeks after they set off for Ireland, Charlotte sent instructions to Martha about their imminent return. The pattern of Charlotte's life had changed. As she wrote to Miss Wooler in September:

> MY OWN LIFE is more occupied than it used to be. I have not so much time for thinking: I am obliged to be more practical, for my dear Arthur is very practical as well as a very punctual and methodical man … Of course he often finds a little work for his wife to do, and I hope she is not sorry to help him. I believe it is not bad for me that his bent should be so wholly towards matters of life and active usefulness, so little inclined to the literary and contemplative … I have [not] been wearied or oppressed; but the fact is my time is not my own now; somebody else wants a good portion of it and says 'We must do so and so'. We do so and so, accordingly; and it generally seems the right thing.

HAWORTH OLD RECTORY.

ABOVE *Haworth Parsonage and churchyard, probably photographed in the 1860s after the death of Patrick Brontë but before the house was altered by the addition of a new gable wing in 1879. Patrick Brontë, his wife Maria, his daughters Charlotte and Emily, and his son Branwell lie buried at Haworth – Anne's grave is at Scarborough, where she died. The Victorian poet Matthew Arnold wrote an elegy to 'Haworth Churchyard', a place of pilgrimage for Brontë lovers from all over the world, which gives the Brontës their epitaph: '… a course Short, yet redoubled by fame …'*

Charlotte had managed to find time to start her fourth novel, *Emma* (though her 'idiot child', *The Professor*, had still not been published, and would not be until two years after her death), but she was to be a wife scarcely nine months. In February 1855, she penned a desperate note to Amelia Ringrose:

> LET ME SPEAK the plain truth – my sufferings are very great – my nights indescribable – sickness with scarce a reprieve – If you can send me anything that will do good – *do* … As to my husband – my heart is knit to him – he is so tender, so good, helpful, patient.

On 31 March 1855 Arthur wrote to Ellen Nussey, 'Our dear Charlotte is no more. She died last night of exhaustion.' The cause of Charlotte's death was given as pthisis (tuberculosis) – the same cause of death as her mother, her sisters and her brother, though in Charlotte's case it may have been partly hastened by complications in early pregnancy. Patrick Brontë wrote to Charlotte's publisher:

> I THANK YOU for your kind sympathy. Having heard my daughter speak so much about you and your family, your letter seemed to be from an old friend. Her husband's sorrow and mine is indeed very great.

Harriet Martineau wrote a generous tribute:

> 'CURRER BELL IS DEAD! The early death of the large family of whom she was sole survivor prepared all who knew the circumstances to expect the loss of this gifted creature at any time: but not the less deep will be the grief of society that her genius will yield us nothing more. We have three works from her pen which will hold their place in the literature of our country; and, but for our frail health, there might have been three times three – for she was under forty [Charlotte was thirty-eight when she died] – and her genius was not of an exhaustible kind.

Whilst Mrs Gaskell, who would be charged by Patrick Brontë to write the biography of his daughter and her friend, reflected on the domestic reality:

> THE SOLEMN TOLLING of Haworth church bell spoke forth the fact of her death to the villagers who had known her from a child, and whose hearts shivered within them as they thought of the two sitting desolate and alone in the old grey house.

The Reverend Patrick Brontë, father, and the Reverend Arthur Bell Nicholls, husband, were to remain in the silent Parsonage for the next six years, 'still *ever near* but *ever separate*', according to the sexton, John Brown, for Nicholls looked after Charlotte's father in compliance with her last wish, until Patrick died, aged eighty-four, in June 1861, the longest-lived of all his family.

FAMILY AND FRIENDS

Tabitha (Tabby) Akroyd Cook and maid-of-all-work in the Brontë household from 1824 until her death in 1855.

Acton Bell *Nom de plume* Anne Brontë used to write under for her published works.

Ellis Bell *Nom de plume* adopted by Emily Brontë.

Currer Bell Charlotte Brontë's *nom de plume* as an author.

Elizabeth Branwell Maria Brontë's sister. 1815–16 stayed at Thornton with Brontës; 1820–1 returned during Maria's fatal illness; moved into the Parsonage to superintend the household and look after the children; d. 29 October 1842.

Anne Brontë b. 17 January 1820; 1835–7 pupil at Roe Head School; 1839 governess to Ingham family, Blake Hall, Mirfield; 1840–5 governess to children of Reverend and Mrs Robinson at Thorp Green Hall, Little Ouseburn; 1846 *Poems* of Currer, Ellis and Acton Bell published; 1847 *Agnes Grey* published; 1848 *The Tenant of Wildfell Hall* published; d. 28 May 1849.

Charlotte Brontë b. 21 April 1816; August 1824–June 1825 pupil at Cowan Bridge School; January 1831–May 1832 pupil at Roe Head School; July 1835–May 1838 teacher at Roe Head School; June–July 1839 governess with Sidgwick family at Stonegappe, near Skipton; March–December 1841 governess to White children at Rawdon, near Bradford; February–November 1842 pupil at Pensionnat Heger, Brussels; January 1843–January 1844 returns to Brussels; 1846 *Poems* of Currer, Ellis and Acton Bell published; 1847 *Jane Eyre* published; 1849 *Shirley* published; 1852 Reverend Arthur Bell Nicholls proposed marriage; 1853 *Villette* published; June 1854 Charlotte married Arthur Bell Nicholls; d. 31 March 1855; 1857 *The Professor* published.

Elizabeth Brontë b. 8 February 1815; July 1824–May 1825 pupil at Cowan Bridge School; d. 15 June 1825.

Emily Jane Brontë b. 30 July 1818; November 1824–June 1825 pupil at Cowan Bridge School; July–October 1835 pupil at Roe Head School; 1836–? teacher at Law Hill School, Halifax; February–November 1842 pupil at Pensionnat Heger, Brussels; 1846 *Poems* of Currer, Ellis and Acton Bell published; 1847 *Wuthering Heights* published; d. 19 December 1848.

Maria Brontë (*née* **Branwell**) b. 1785 Penzance, Cornwall; 29 December 1812 married the Reverend Patrick Brontë; 1814–1820 six children, Maria, Elizabeth, Charlotte, Branwell, Emily and Anne, born; d. 15 September 1821.

Maria Brontë b. 1814 (christened 23 April); 1824–5 pupil at Cowan Bridge School; d. 6 May 1825.

The Reverend Patrick Brontë b. 17 March 1777 Co. Down; 1802–6 student at St John's College, Cambridge; 21 December 1807 ordained in Church of England; published *Cottage Poems* (1811); *The Rural Minstrel* (1813); *The Cottage in the Wood or The Art of Becoming Rich and Happy* (1815); *The Maid of Killarney* (1818); *The Phenomenon* (1824); 29 December 1829 married Maria Branwell at Guiseley Church, near Bradford, whilst curate at Hartshead; May 1815 curate at Thornton; February 1820 appointed to living at Haworth; April 1820 Brontë family move into Parsonage, Haworth; *The Sign of the Times* (1835); d. 7 June 1861.

Patrick Branwell Brontë b. 26 June 1817; 1835 went to London to enrol in Royal Academy Schools, failed and returned home; 1838 went to Bradford as a portrait painter; 1839–40 tutor to Postlethwaite family, Ulverston; August 1840 assistant clerk at Sowerby Bridge Railway Station; 1841 promoted to chief clerk at Luddenden Foot Railway Station; 1842 sacked for 'irregularities'; January 1843 tutor to Robinson family, Thorp Green Hall; July 1845 dismissed; d. 24 September 1848.

John Brown Sexton to Patrick Brontë, master of Haworth Masonic Lodge and friend and confidant of Branwell; d. 1855.

Martha Brown Daughter of John Brown. b. 1828; came to work at the Parsonage on washdays at the age of 10, and later joined the household as a servant. She was one of Mrs Gaskell's sources for her *Life* of Charlotte.

Jane Fennell Cousin of Maria Brontë. Married Patrick Brontë's friend, Reverend William Morgan; d. 1827.

John Fennell Father of Jane, uncle of Maria Brontë; headmaster of Woodhouse Grove Academy near Bradford. 1812 Maria met Patrick Brontë for the first time while staying with the Fennells.

Elizabeth Firth b. 1797; 1815 welcomed Brontës to Thornton on their arrival and families became close friends; Patrick proposed marriage after Maria's death; she declined; September 1825 married the Reverend James Franks, vicar of Huddersfield; continued to take an interest in the welfare of the Brontë children until her death in September 1837.

Nancy Garrs 1816 nurse to the Brontë children after Charlotte's birth; 1824 left to get married.

Sarah Garrs Younger sister of Nancy. 1818 joined the Brontë household; 1824 left with her sister.

Elizabeth Cleghorn Gaskell (1810–65). Novelist. 1832 married the Unitarian minister William Gaskell; mother of four daughters; August 1850 met Charlotte Brontë and visited Haworth; Charlotte stayed several times at Gaskell's home at Plymouth Grove, Manchester; author of *Mary Barton* (originally called *John Barton*, 1848), *Ruth* (1853) and *North and South* (1855), all novels concerned to expose social problems during the height of the Industrial Revolution. Also wrote *Cranford* (1851–3), *Sylvia's Lovers*, (1863) and *Wives and Daughters* (1866). Her *Life of Charlotte Brontë*, written at Patrick Brontë's request, was published in 1857.

John Greenwood Stationer at Haworth. Kept a journal which has proved an illuminating source for the lives of the Brontës.

Francis Henry Grundy Railway engineer on Halifax–Leeds railway. 1841 met Branwell at Luddenden Foot, became friends; 1879 Grundy's recollections of Branwell – who he believed wrote most of *Wuthering Heights* – were published in *Pictures of the Past*.

Constantin Heger (b. 1809) and **Claire Zoë Heger** (*née* **Parent**, b. 1804) 1834 Constantin's wife and child died in the cholera epidemic; met Zoë Parent, who had established a girls' school at 32 rue d'Isabelle after the 1830 revolution, while he was a teacher at the Athenée Royal, a leading Brussels boys' school; 1836 married, and had six children. February–November 1842 Charlotte and Emily were pupils at the Pensionnat Heger, where M. Heger also taught; January 1843–January 1844 Charlotte returned to Brussels as a teacher and pupil. On her return to Haworth she wrote a number of imploring letters to M. Heger; Mrs Gaskell was shown these letters by M. Heger when she visited Brussels whilst researching her *Life* of Charlotte. Charlotte drew on M. Heger for her portrait of Paul Emmanuel in *Villette*, and portrayed Mme Heger – who realized that Charlotte had conceived a passion for her husband – as Zoraide Reuter in *The Professor* and Mme Beck in *Villette*.

Ingham family 1839 Anne was governess to their children at Blake Hall, Mirfield; she drew on her experiences there in *Agnes Grey*.

Reverend Evan Jenkins Resident chaplain of the Chapel Royal, Brussels. Advised on suitable schools for Charlotte and Emily; he and his wife tried to entertain the reclusive Brontë sisters during their time at the Pensionnat Heger.

Sir James Kay Shuttleworth (1804–77) A medical doctor whose experience in the great cholera epidemic in Manchester in 1832 led him to campaign for improved living conditions for the poor, parliamentary reform and the repeal of the Corn Laws: he introduced a national system of education and teacher training; 1839–40 established the first teacher-training college in Battersea and introduced the system of school inspectors and pupil-teacher training. August 1850 Charlotte first met Mrs Gaskell whilst staying at the Windermere holiday home of Sir James and Lady Kay Shuttleworth.

George Henry Lewes Critic, editor, essayist, novelist, biographer of Goethe and writer in the natural sciences; 1854 until death common-law husband of Mary Ann Evans (George Eliot). Lewes reviewed

Charlotte's novels; she asked her publisher, 'Can you give me any information respecting Mr Lewes? what station he occupies in the literary world and what works he has written?'; once this had been established to her satisfaction the two corresponded vigorously.

Joseph Bentley Leyland (1811–51) Sculptor, son of the sometime editor of the *Halifax Guardian*, brother of Francis, and antiquarian. Studied under Benjamin Robert Haydon in London; 1832 exhibited in Manchester; returned to Halifax and became friend, drinking companion and creditor of Branwell; 1886 *The Brontë Family with special reference to Patrick Branwell Brontë* published.

Harriet Martineau Political economist, writer and free thinker. Her 25-volume tract on economic questions, *Illustrations of Political Economy*, was immensely popular; also wrote novels, including *Deerbrook* (1839), and published her autobiography in 1855. Charlotte was anxious to make the acquaintance of this powerful writer on a range of contemporary concerns – slavery, education and women's rights – and visited her in London and in the Lake District. Martineau's critical review of *Villette* terminated the friendship, but she wrote an acclamatory obituary on Charlotte's death.

The Reverend William Morgan (d. 1858) Fellow curate with Patrick Brontë in Shropshire; 1829 married Jane Fennell in a joint ceremony with Patrick and Maria; lifelong friend of Patrick, officiating at the funeral of Maria and christening and burying his children. Dr Thomas Boultby in *Shirley* draws on Morgan.

T. C. Newby Publisher, Cavendish Square, London. Published *Agnes Grey* and the *Tenant of Wildfell Hall* by Anne Brontë, and Emily Brontë's *Wuthering Heights*; tried to pass off the *Tenant of Wildfell Hall* as being by the same author as *Jane Eyre*.

Arthur Bell Nicholls (1818–1906). b. Co. Antrim; educated Trinity College, Dublin; Puseyite clergyman; 1845 came as a curate to Haworth; 1854 married Charlotte and remained at Haworth until Patrick's death in 1861 when he returned to Ireland, married his cousin and became a farmer. Jealous guardian of Charlotte's literary reputation and source of much archival material relating to the Brontë family.

Ellen Nussey (1817–1897) Youngest of thirteen children of a Yorkshire cloth manufacturer. 1831 met Charlotte at Roe Head School and a lifelong friendship and correspondence ensued; never married or worked outside the home. Her brother, Henry, a clergyman, proposed marriage to Charlotte in 1839, was rejected, and probably served as a model for St John Rivers in *Jane Eyre*.

The Misses Patchett Kept a school at Law Hill, Halifax, where Emily taught for a time after 1836.

Amelia Ringrose At one time engaged to Ellen Nussey's brother, George; married Mary Taylor's brother, Joe; friend and correspondent of Charlotte; visited Haworth.

Robinson family 1841–5 Anne and Branwell Brontë employed as governess and tutor respectively to the children of the Reverend Edmund Robinson and his wife Lydia at Thorp Green Hall. Mrs Gaskell's revelations about the relationship between Mrs Robinson and Branwell in her *Life* of Charlotte led to a threatened lawsuit by Lydia Robinson (by then Lady Scott – she had remarried after her husband's death) and the first edition was withdrawn.

George Murray Smith (b. 1824) Head of the publishing firm Smith, Elder & Co., 65 Cornhill, London, a large and respectable house which had published Ruskin's early work, Browning, Thackeray and much of Matthew Arnold. He became Charlotte's publisher and friend; she maintained a frequent correspondence; he treated her most hospitably on her visits to London.

Robert Southey (1774–1843) Poet laureate from 1813. Friend of Coleridge and Wordsworth with whom he shared revolutionary ardour in the early stages of the French Revolution. Wrote long heroic epics ('Thalaba' (1801), 'Madoc' (1805)); his best remembered poem is probably 'After the Battle of Blenheim'; also wrote history, a life of Nelson (1813) and of Wesley (1820). Moved decisively to the right in political outlook; 1821 Byron attacked him as a hack and political renegade in *The Vision of Judgement*; 1817 Thomas Love Peacock satirized him as Mr Feathernest in *Melincourt*. 1836 Charlotte wrote soliciting his advice on her poetry; she received the advice: 'literature cannot be the business of a woman's life.'

James Taylor Employee of the publishing firm Smith, Elder & Co.; 1851 opened an office for the company in India and proposed that Charlotte should accompany him as his wife; she declined.

Mary Taylor (1817–93) 1831 met Charlotte at Roe Head School; subsequently Charlotte visited the Red House, Gomersal, where the Taylor family lived. Joshua Taylor was a cloth manufacturer and banker in straitened circumstances; Mary shared his radical views. Mary and her sister Martha – another friend from Roe Head days – encouraged Charlotte to join them in Belgium to further her education; Martha died there. Mary continued studies in Germany; 1845 emigrated to New Zealand, opened a store in Wellington and prospered. On her return to England, published *The First Duty of Women* (1885), *Swiss Notes*, and a novel, *Miss Miles* (1890). She and Charlotte wrote frequently to each other; Mary destroyed the letters, but provided vivid insights for Mrs Gaskell's *Life*. The Yorke family in *Shirley* owe a considerable debt to the Taylors, with Rose modelled on Mary, Jessy on Martha, Hiram on Joshua and Hester on Mrs Taylor.

William Makepeace Thackeray (1811–63) Novelist, journalist and satirical observer of metropolitan manners. Wrote for *Fraser's Magazine* (to which he contributed *The Yellow Plush Correspondence*), and *Punch* (to which he contributed the parodies *The Snobs of England*); from 1860 he edited and contributed to *The Cornhill Magazine*. His books include *Catherine* (1839), *The Luck of Barry Lyndon* (1844), *The Rose and the Ring* (for children, 1855) and, the most famous, *Vanity Fair* (1847–8). Charlotte admired him greatly and dedicated the second edition of *Jane Eyre* to him. On making his acquaintance, however, she found him glib and unworthy, and, whilst he admired her work, Thackeray found Charlotte dull and over-earnest.

William Weightman 1839 arrived as curate at Haworth – of the many curates who served Patrick Brontë, the most warmly remembered: Patrick admired him, Charlotte found him, 'bonny, pleasant … careless, fickle, unclerical', Anne may have fallen in love with him, and he became a good friend to Branwell – d. 6 September 1842, of cholera.

Charles (1707–88) and **John** (1703–91) **Wesley** Co-founders of the Evangelical or Methodist movement in the Church of England. The revival was strong in Yorkshire and Lancashire and an important influence on the religious views of Patrick Brontë and his family.

William Smith Williams A reader for Smith, Elder & Co. who first recognized the strength of Charlotte's writing. 1848 met her when she arrived at the office with Anne to reveal the true identity of Currer, Ellis and Acton Bell; became her friend and correspondent.

Laetitia Wheelwright One of the five daughters of Dr Thomas Wheelwright and his wife who attended the Pensionnat Heger at the same time as Charlotte and Emily. Emily taught music to the younger ones; Laetitia, who disliked Emily, became a friend of Charlotte's and they wrote to each other on their return to England.

The Reverend Carus Wilson Clergyman, writer and philanthropist, vicar of Tunstall, Yorkshire, and founder of Cowan Bridge School for Daughters of the Clergy. 1824 Maria, Elizabeth, Charlotte and Emily were sent there; Maria and Elizabeth died as a result. Mrs Gaskell's *Life* of Charlotte made clear that Lowood in *Jane Eyre* was modelled on Cowan Bridge and the Reverend Brocklehurst on Carus Wilson; much controversy ensued.

Margaret Wooler (1792–1885) Headmistress of Roe Head School; later moved to Dewsbury Moor, Yorkshire. Charlotte, Emily and Anne attended as pupils; 1835–8 Charlotte returned as a teacher. Charlotte grew to admire Miss Wooler and the two corresponded frequently; 1854 she gave Charlotte away at her wedding to Arthur Bell Nicholls.

IN THE FOOTSTEPS OF THE BRONTËS

HAWORTH, NEAR KEIGHLEY, WEST YORKSHIRE

Main Street Most of the houses in Main Street date from the eighteenth and early nineteenth centuries. They were built for cottage-industry textile workers and their families, with rows of narrow windows giving sufficient light for the operation of hand-looms. In the 1840s, domestic cloth production reached a peak in Haworth with over 1,200 looms in operation in the neighbourhood.

The architecture of Main Street is much as it was during the Brontës' time at Haworth – though many buildings have been converted to cater for the tourist trade – and the cobbled street with its stone horizontal 'setts', which prevented horses from slipping down the steep hill, remains today.

Black Bull Hotel An eighteenth-century inn where Branwell Brontë spent much of his time drinking. He was a favourite with the landlord, who would often send for the Parson's talented son to amuse his guests with his wit and learning. It remains a licensed inn.

Druggist's Store (opposite the Black Bull Hotel, now a gift shop) Where Branwell obtained his supplies of laudanum, to which he grew increasingly addicted.

The Parsonage Built in 1779 for the incumbent of St Michael and All Angels. The Reverend Patrick Brontë, his wife Maria, his son Branwell, and his daughters Maria, Elizabeth, Charlotte, Emily and Anne moved into the Parsonage in 1820; Patrick lived there until his death in 1861. The house is a traditional Georgian design of Yorkshire sandstone, darkened by the industrial smoke. The Parsonage has been extensively altered since the Brontës lived there – notably by the addition of a north and a west wing – but its central aspect is unchanged and visitors can look at rooms which are arranged and furnished much as they were in the Brontës' lifetime. After the deaths of Branwell, Emily and Anne between 1848 and 1849, Charlotte had some alterations carried out to the house: the dining-room and a bedroom were enlarged at the expense of the hall and the nursery, and in 1854 Charlotte arranged for a storeroom to be converted into a study for her husband, the Reverend Arthur Bell Nicholls.

St Michael and All Angels Parish Church Only the tower remains of the old church in which Patrick Brontë – and the great Evangelical minister William Grimshaw before him – preached. The rest of the building was demolished in 1879 and the present building was dedicated two years later.

Except for Anne, who is buried at Scarborough, all the Brontës lie buried in a vault beneath the church; an inscription near the chancel steps marks the vault and also indicates where the Brontës' pew stood in the old church. A wall monument to the Brontës carved by the church sexton and friend of Branwell's John Brown, is now in the church's *Brontë Memorial Chapel*, which was completed in 1964, and a tablet to William Weightman, Patrick Brontë's popular curate and a friend of his children, is on the wall facing the font. The top tier of the three-tier pulpit from which Patrick preached is still in use at Stanbury Church in the moorland village some mile and a half from Haworth along the Colne road.

The Churchyard More than 40,000 residents of Haworth and its environs are reputed to be buried here. Near the Parsonage wall are the graves of two of the Brontës' servants, Tabitha Ackroyd and Martha Brown. The gate in the garden wall (now blocked up, but marked by a stone inscription) led from the Parsonage garden into the graveyard and it was through this that the coffins of the Brontës were carried to their funerals.

Brontë Falls (2 miles from the Parsonage) So named for this was a favourite moorland walk of Charlotte, Emily and Anne to a tributary of Sladen Beck. Spanning the beck below the falls is a slab bridge, now known as *Brontë Bridge* since it is a replica of the one the Brontës would have known; a natural rock in the shape of a chair has become known as the *Brontë Seat* and it is reputed that, sitting here, Charlotte wrote some of her poetry.

Brookroyd House (on the Birstall–Batley border) Ellen Nussey moved to Brookroyd in 1836. Charlotte visited and corresponded with her here for the rest of her life.

Cowan Bridge (2 miles south-east of Kirby Lonsdale, on the A65 Settle–Kendal road) In July 1824 Elizabeth and Maria Brontë were sent to board at the Reverend Carus Wilson's new school 'for daughters of the impoverished clergy' housed in a row of converted cottages. The harsh regime and miasmic surroundings of the school led to the deaths of Maria and Elizabeth, and Charlotte and Emily were removed in 1825. In *Jane Eyre*, Charlotte portrayed Cowan Bridge as Lowood and *Tunstall Church* (2 miles to the south-east, on the A683 Lancaster Road) as Brocklebridge Church, where the unfortunate inmates of the school had to trudge every Sunday to hear the Reverend Brocklehurst (Carus Wilson) preach.

Gawthorpe Hall, Padiham (3 miles north-west of Burnley, on the A671) Charlotte visited this imposing three-storey Tudor building, altered to the specifications of Sir Charles Barry, in 1850 at the invitation of Sir James and Lady Kay Shuttleworth. In January 1855 she paid another visit with her husband, Arthur Bell Nicholls, who had been offered the incumbency of Kay Shuttleworth's new church at Padiham. Nicholls refused since he and Charlotte felt committed to stay at Haworth during Patrick Brontë's lifetime.

Gomersal: The Red House (on the A65 Bradford–Dewsbury Road) Home of Charlotte's schoolfriends Mary and Martha Taylor, this unusual house, constructed of brick rather than Yorkshire stone, was built *c*.1600. Charlotte, who was a frequent visitor, used it as a model for 'Briarmains' in *Shirley* and the Taylor family as a model for the Yorke family. Mary Taylor's radical father, Joshua – Charlotte's model for the character Hiram Yorke – was the owner of a large woollen mill at Hunsworth, two miles away, which Charlotte renamed Hollow Mill in *Shirley*.

Guiseley: St Oswald's Parish Church (5 miles north-east of Bradford, just off the A65 Leeds–Skipton road) The church where, on 29 December 1812, the Reverend Patrick Brontë married Maria Branwell in a double ceremony in which Maria's cousin, Jane Fennell, married Patrick's friend, the Reverend William Morgan. The two clergymen officiated at each other's ceremony, and John Fennell gave both brides away.

Hartshead: St Peter's Parish Church (on the B6119) Patrick Brontë was curate of St Peter's, Hartshead-cum-Clifton, between 1811 and 1815, and Maria, the Brontës' first child, was baptized there on 23 April 1814. Nunnely Church in *Shirley* is modelled on St Peter's, and Nunnely itself on Hartshead village.

Hathersage (11 miles south-west of Sheffield, on the A625) Henry Nussey, Ellen's brother, was appointed vicar of Hathersage in 1845 and in June–July that year Charlotte spent a fortnight there with Ellen. Hathersage is portrayed as Morton in *Jane Eyre* and it is probable that Charlotte took the name Jane Eyre from the commemorative brasses in the church of the Eyre family of *North Lees Hall*, near Hathersage.

Hightown (west of Liversedge, on the A649 Halifax–Liversedge road) Whilst curate at Hartshead, the Brontës rented a house in *Clough Lane* where Maria was born in 1813 and Elizabeth in 1815. There were Luddite disturbances at nearby *Liversedge* during Patrick's time here, and Charlotte depicted this social unrest in the Spen valley in *Shirley*.

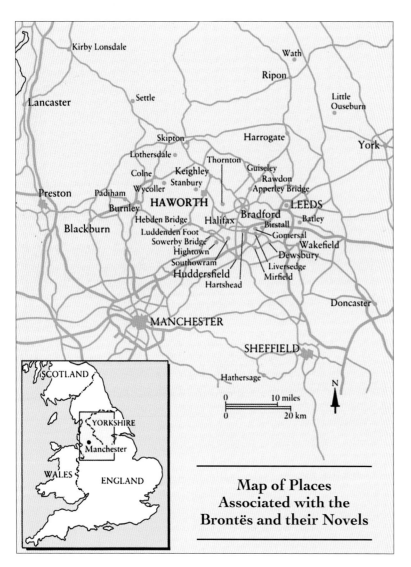

Map of Places Associated with the Brontës and their Novels

Law Hill, Southowram (2 miles south-east of Halifax, off the A58) In September 1837, Emily went as a teacher to the Misses Patchett's exclusive boarding school for girls, opened in 1825. It is not known how long Emily remained at Law Hill, but about 6 months seems likely. The imposing seventeenth-century mansion of *High Sunderland Hall* nearby, overlooking the beautiful Shibden Valley, was also probably a part-model for Wuthering Heights.

Luddenden Foot (in the Calder Valley, just off the A646 Halifax–Hebden Bridge road) Branwell was a clerk for the Leeds–Manchester Railway Company at Luddenden Foot from April 1841 until his dismissal in March 1842. He spent a great deal of time drinking with his friends in the *Nelson Inn*, Luddenden village, about half a mile away. Although the station has been demolished, the inn remains largely unchanged.

Norton Conyers (3½ miles north of Ripon, on the A61 to Wath) A Jacobean House which Charlotte visited whilst she was a governess at Stonegappe. It is thought that the story of Mrs Rochester, 'the mad woman in the attic', derives from features of the house and a story of the Graham family who had lived at Norton Conyers since 1624.

Oakwell Hall, Birstall (off the A652 Bradford–Batley road) A stone manor house built in 1583. Charlotte frequently visited the house when staying with Ellen and it provided the inspiration for Shirley Keeldar's house, Fieldhead, in *Shirley*.

Ponden Hall (3 miles from Haworth, on the Colne Road) Built in 1634, the house was rebuilt in 1801 and has been extended more recently. It was the model for Thrushcross Grange in *Wuthering Heights*, leased by Mr Lockwood from Heathcliff.

Ponden Kirk (about 2 miles outside Stanbury, in the direction of Colne) A prominent and very isolated rock outcrop, the inspiration for Penistone Crag in *Wuthering Heights*.

Roe Head, Mirfield (just off the A62 Huddersfield–Leeds road, on the B6119 to Hartshead) Charlotte Brontë was sent to Miss Wooler's school at Roe Head in January 1831 when she was 14. It was here that she met her lifelong friends, Ellen Nussey and Mary Taylor. Charlotte left Roe Head in July 1832, to return as a teacher in 1835 with Emily and then Anne as pupils.

The Rydings, Birstall (at Birstall Smithies, close to the A62/A652 Leeds–Bradford roads) Charlotte first visited her friend Ellen Nussey's family home in September 1832, taken by her brother Branwell, who thought it 'paradise'. Mr Rochester's house, Thornfield Hall, in *Jane Eyre* is partly based on the battlemented, early eighteenth-century house.

Scarborough Anne Brontë visited Scarborough several times between 1841 and 1845 whilst she was a governess at Thorp Green Hall, and the resort is portrayed in her first novel, *Agnes Grey*. Charlotte and Ellen Nussey brought Anne to Scarborough to seek a cure for her mortal illness in May 1849. She died there at 2 The Cliff (now occupied by the *Grand Hotel* on St Nicholas's Cliff), and is buried in the churchyard of *St Mary's Parish Church* – the only member of the Brontë family not to lie at Haworth. Charlotte also greatly liked the sea: she visited *Filey* in 1849 and 1852, *Bridlington* in 1839 and 1849, and *Hornsea* in 1853.

Sowerby Bridge (in the Calder Valley, between Halifax and Hebden Bridge, on the A646) Branwell was appointed clerk at Sowerby Bridge station on the new Leeds–Manchester railway in August 1840. He was transferred to Luddenden Foot the following April.

Stonegappe Hall, Lothersdale (4 miles west of Cross Hills, off the A6068 Keighley–Colne road) Charlotte had a position as a governess to the Sidgwick children at Stonegappe Hall between May and July 1839, and later portrayed the house as Gateshead Hall in *Jane Eyre*.

Top (or High) Withens (3 miles west of Haworth) A remote Elizabethan farmhouse high on the Pennine Way, the inspiration for Heathcliff's home in *Wuthering Heights*.

Thornton (4 miles west of Bradford, on the B6145) Patrick Brontë was curate at Thornton from 1815 to 1820 and it was at 74 Market Street that Charlotte (1816), Branwell (1817), Emily (1818) and Anne (1820) were born. The *parish church* contains the font where the children were baptized. *Kipping House*, where Elizabeth Firth often entertained the Brontës to tea, is in Lower Kipping Lane.

Thorp Green Hall, Little Ouseburn (10 miles north-west of York, on the B6265) Anne went to Thorp Green as a governess to the Robinson children in May 1840. In January 1843 she was joined by Branwell who was employed as a tutor until his dismissal in June or July 1845. Anne also resigned.

Woodhouse Grove School, Apperley Bridge (4 miles north of Bradford, on the A658 Harrogate road) Maria Branwell came to Woodhouse Grove in July 1812 when she was 29 to stay with her uncle, John Fennell, who was headmaster of the boarding school for sons of Methodist ministers. It was here that Maria and Patrick Branwell met through Fennell's daughter, Jane, who was engaged to Patrick's friend, the Reverend William Morgan.

Wycoller (2½ miles south-east of Colne) The ruins of Wycoller Hall were reputedly Charlotte's inspiration for Ferndean in *Jane Eyre*. The hamlet has been designated a country park.

INDEX

THE SOURCES

The standard general edition of the Brontë letters is the four-volume *The Brontës: Their Lives, Friendships and Correspondence*, edited by T. J. Wise and J. A. Symington (The Shakespeare Head, Oxford, 1932). However, it contains omissions and inaccuracies, and a definitive edition of the letters edited by Margaret Smith was published in 2007. See also: *The Miscellaneous and Unpublished Writings of Charlotte and Branwell Brontë*, edited by T. J. Wise and J. A. Symington (1934); *The Brontës' Life and Letters*, Clemence Shorter (1908); and *An Edition of the Early Writings of Charlotte Brontë*, Christine Alexander (2 volumes, 1987, 1991). Major collections of the Brontë manuscripts, letters, juvenilia, etc. are held in the Brontë Parsonage Museum at Haworth, the Brotherton Library, Leeds, the Fitzwilliam Museum, Cambridge, and the British Library, and there are several collections in the USA (*see* particularly the Bonnell Collection, Philadelphia).

The *Transactions of the Brontë Society* is the main periodical devoted to Brontë studies, and texts of recently discovered letters etc. are published here.

ACKNOWLEDGEMENTS

The illustrations are reproduced by kind permission of the following: Birmingham City Museum & Art Gallery 107; Bradford City Art Gallery (Bridgeman Art Library) 79; Bridgeman Art Library 34, 63, 110/11, 123, 127; Trustees of the British Library 8/9, 98, 100/1, 108, 113, 118/19, 141; Trustees of the British Museum, frontispiece; Brontë Parsonage Museum 10, 11, 12, 20/1, 23 (both), 24, 26, 28, 29, 31, 32, 33, 36, 36/7, 38, 39, 40, 41, 42, 43, 44, 48, 49, 51, 52 (left), 53 (both), 54, 56, 57, 61, 62, 64, 65, 67, 69, 70, 72, 72/3, 78, 80, 80/1, 89, 90, 92, 94, 95, 96, 102, 103, 104, 105, 108/9, 112, 116, 117, 119, 120, 130, 131, 142, 144 (both), 147 (both), 148; Calderdale Leisure Services, Bankfield Museum, Halifax 75; Mary Evans Picture Library 136; Fine Art Society, London 134; Guildhall Library 120/1; Leeds City Art Gallery (photo Courtauld Institute of Art, Witt Library) 25; Philippa Lewis 44, 91, 124/5; Manchester Central Library 139; Mansell Collection 16, 17, 45, 52 (right), 76, 84, 87, 115, 132, 146; Museum of London 135; National Maritime Museum 83; National Portrait Gallery, London 7, 71, 114, 126, 137 (both); Collection Monsieur René Pechère 99; Ulster Museum, Belfast 15; Victoria & Albert Museum 58; The Wordsworth Trust, Dove Cottage 138; York City Art Gallery 143.

These illustrations came from the following books: R. Ackermann, *A History of the University of Cambridge* (1815) 19, 20; R. Ayton and W. Daniell, *Voyage Round Great Britain, Volume VIII* (1814–1825) 22; *Life and Works of Charlotte Brontë and her Sisters* (1872–3), illustrations by E. M. Wimperis 32/3, 40/1, 68/9, 86, 88, 93, 112/ 13, 128, 132/3, 140/1; A. Thornton, *Don Juan in London* (1836) 70/1; George Walker, *The Costume of Yorkshire* (1814) 27, 47.

The map was produced by Eugene Fleury.

I am most grateful to the assistant curator and librarian at the Brontë Parsonage Museum, Haworth, Kathryn White, and her assistant, Tracey Messenger, for their invaluable help and advice. I would also like to thank Gillian Hawkins for her enthusiasm, Holly Jones for additional research, Sarah Bloxham for her skill and patience as editor, and Philippa Lewis for the wealth of her pictorial knowledge. JULIET GARDINER.